M000308905

Praise for *The Kickstart*
Making GREAT Makerspaces by Laura Fleming

This book is an AMAZING hands-on tool for planning and implementing a culture of making in schools. Laura Fleming provides direction, support, and inspiration for educators starting their journey into making!

Jacie Maslyk, Assistant Superintendent
Hopewell Area School District
Pittsburgh, PA

There are makerspaces and then there are GREAT makerspaces. Laura Fleming, a makerspace pioneer, has written another must-read for anyone wanting to create a great makerspace for their school community. Read this book—and learn from one of the best. Anyone involved in the development of makerspaces will treasure this text because it takes readers on an interactive journey through the process of planning and creating a GREAT makerspace. Look no further than this book.

Eric Sheninger, Senior Fellow
International Center for Leadership in Education (ICLE)
Cypress, TX

"Making" is a powerful way to engage students and observe their learning process with the product as evidence. Creating space for that to happen is "making space" for our 21st century learners.

Jill Berkowicz, Author, Adjunct Professor, Consultant
Corwin, *Education Week*, SUNY New Paltz
Poughkeepsie, NY

In the worlds of makerspaces, nobody speaks with a more credible voice than Laura Fleming. In her highly anticipated second book, Fleming lays out a clear blueprint for those who wish to create a makerspace, and she provides countless inspiring examples that beautifully illustrate what a thriving makerspace looks like in action! A must-have!

Ross Cooper, Supervisor of Instructional Practice K–12
Salisbury Township School District
Allentown, PA

The ideas for makerspaces are easy to follow and could be implemented, in some cases, with little prep. This is a bonus!

Susan E. Schipper, Elementary Educator
Charles Street School
Palmyra, NJ

Laura Fleming's book offers a clear, student-centered, and step-by-step approach for all educators eager to implement "making" in their classrooms or schools. It brings practical information and her experiences to ensure a successful outcome!

Lynne Schrum, PhD, Professor
Nova Southeastern University
Fort Lauderdale, FL

If we are going to prepare tomorrow's problem solvers and innovators, we must empower them to design and create today. In this book, best-selling author Laura Fleming has done it again! This hands-on guide moves readers from brainstorming and planning, to selecting resources, and ultimately, to the needed concrete steps to designing the makerspaces today's modern learners need! This dynamic guide will undoubtedly serve as a centerpiece for your authentic learning toolkit.

Thomas C. Murray, Director of Innovation
Future Ready Schools
Washington, DC

THE
KICKSTART
GUIDE TO MAKING
GREAT
MAKERSPACES

THE
KICKSTART
GUIDE TO MAKING

GREAT
MAKERSPACES

LAURA
FLEMING

CORWIN
A SAGE Publishing Company

FOR INFORMATION:

Corwin

A SAGE Company

2455 Teller Road

Thousand Oaks, California 91320

(800) 233-9936

www.corwin.com

SAGE Publications Ltd.

1 Oliver's Yard

55 City Road

London EC1Y 1SP

United Kingdom

SAGE Publications India Pvt. Ltd.

B 1/I 1 Mohan Cooperative Industrial Area

Mathura Road, New Delhi 110 044

India

SAGE Publications Asia-Pacific Pte. Ltd.

3 Church Street

#10-04 Samsung Hub

Singapore 049483

Acquisitions Editor: Ariel Bartlett

Senior Associate Editor: Desirée A. Bartlett

Editorial Assistant: Kaitlyn Irwin

Production Editor: Melanie Birdsall

Copy Editor: Meg Granger

Typesetter: C&M Digitals (P) Ltd.

Proofreader: Alison Syring

Indexer: Molly Hall

Cover and Interior Designer: Anupama Krishnan

Marketing Manager: Margaret O'Connor

Library of Congress Cataloging-in-Publication Data

Names: Fleming, Laura, author.

Title: The kickstart guide to making great makerspaces / Laura Fleming.

Description: Thousand Oaks, California : Corwin, [2018] | Includes index.

Identifiers: LCCN 2017023936 | ISBN 9781506392523 (spiral : alk. paper)

Subjects: LCSH: Maker movement in education. | Makerspaces.

Classification: LCC LB1029.M35 F54 2018 | DDC 371.39—dc23
LC record available at https://lccn.loc.gov/2017023936

This book is printed on acid-free paper.

SUSTAINABLE FORESTRY INITIATIVE

Certified Chain of Custody
Promoting Sustainable Forestry
www.sfiprogram.org
SFI-01268

SFI label applies to text stock

18 19 20 21 10 9 8 7 6 5 4 3

Contents

Personalized	*Differentiated*
Deep	*Intentional*
Empowering	*Inspiring*
Equitable	

Reflect on your own school experiences, gather your team, and brainstorm your vision for your makerspace. How can making transform school for your students?

Understand
Assess
Consider
Develop
Order

Based on the themes you uncovered in the makerspace planning process, you will stock your makerspace with the materials, resources, and supplies your space needs!

Now that you've completed the makerspace planning process, it is time to consider what making in the makerspace will actually look like. Challenge your students with authentic project ideas, activities, and opportunities for reflection.

How do we assess in a makerspace?

About the Author

www.worldsofmaking.com
www.worlds-of-learning.com
@LFlemingEDU

Laura Fleming has been an educator in the state of New Jersey for 20 years. She has been both a classroom teacher and media specialist in Grades K–8 and is currently a library media specialist for Grades 9–12. She has played a prominent role in education as a writer and speaker and has served as an educational consultant on next-generation teaching methods and tools. Laura cohosts the *Movers & Makers* podcast and is the author of the best-selling *Worlds of Making: Best Practices for Establishing a Makerspace for Your School* (Corwin, 2015).

Laura is also the creator of a digital badge-based professional development platform in which educators all over the world earn badges in acknowledgment of their professional learning. Her library makerspace has garnered national attention and has served as an inspiration for schools across the country. She is also an honoree of the National School Boards Association's "20 to Watch" in educational technology leadership for 2014 and was recently nominated as a White House Champion of Change for Making.

Laura is also the creator of the Worlds of Making Digital Academy, which provides makerspace professional development for teachers. Her goal is to create learning experiences that empower and equip students with necessary skills to effectively produce and consume content across multiple media platforms. She is also driven to enable educators and cohorts in applying these innovative methods and cutting-edge technology in their fields of expertise. Laura is an educational consultant, thought leader, and speaker on education, librarianship, and technology.

Acknowledgments

Corwin gratefully acknowledges the contributions of the following reviewers:

Patricia Allanson, Seventh-Grade Intensive Math Instructor
Deltona Middle School
Deltona, FL

Marsha Basanda, Fifth-Grade Teacher
Monarch Elementary
Simpsonville, SC

Carol S. Holzberg, Director of Technology
Greenfield Public Schools
Greenfield, MA

Marti Hooten, Second-Grade Teacher
Leaphart Elementary School
Columbia, SC

Susan E. Schipper, Elementary Educator
Charles Street School
Palmyra, NJ

Margie Zamora, Digital Learning Coach/Instructional Technology Support
Elaine Wynn Elementary School
Las Vegas, NV

Let's build the change we wish to see.

—Emily Pilloton, Educator/Designer

GIVE THE PUPILS SOMETHING TO DO, NOT SOMETHING TO LEARN; AND THE DOING IS OF SUCH A NATURE AS TO DEMAND THINKING; LEARNING NATURALLY RESULTS.

—JOHN DEWEY

IN A MAKERSPACE, STUDENTS GET TO MAKE THEIR OWN MEANING.

—KAREN CHESER, EDUCATOR

Play is the highest form of research.

—Albert Einstein

The best tool I've found for my maker programs is saying "Yes" or "Try it and see."

—Holly Stork-Post, Children's Librarian

Makers dream big, take risks, explore options, imagine new possibilities, show courage, express creativity, and embrace challenge.

—Krissy Venosdale, Educator

tinker, create, make, and do.

Schools have a responsibility to expose kids to things they don't yet know they love.

—Gary Stager, Educator/Author

TO INVENT, YOU NEED A GOOD IMAGINATION AND A PILE OF JUNK.

—THOMAS EDISON

The "maker movement" leads to a new pedagogy— "Tinkquiry"—Tinkering + Inquiry.

—Peter Skillen and Brenda Sherry, Educators

When we allow children to experiment, take risks, and play with their own ideas, we give them permission to trust themselves.

—Sylvia Martinez, Educator/Author

INNOVATION IS A PROCESS, NOT A PRODUCT.

—GEORGE COUROS, EDUCATOR/AUTHOR

MAKER MANIFESTO

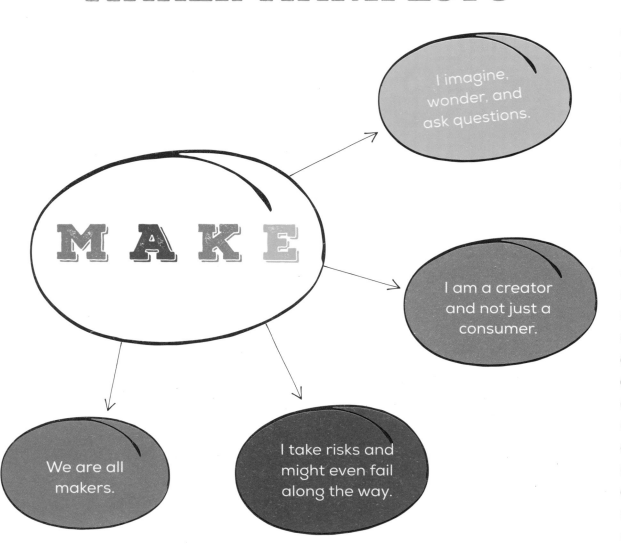

MAKE

I imagine, wonder, and ask questions.

I am a creator and not just a consumer.

We are all makers.

I take risks and might even fail along the way.

THE KICKSTART GUIDE TO MAKING GREAT MAKERSPACES

Introduction

"There are many ways to make a makerspace. But the best way to make it is . . ."

These are the words from my son Gavin, 8 at the time, when I told him I was going to be writing this new book, and his suggestion for how it should begin. So that is where we are beginning. Anyone can create a makerspace, but it is my hope that this book will help you make your makerspace the best it can be.

There are makerspaces, and then there are GREAT makerspaces! This new book is aimed to support ALL educators as they plan and create GREAT makerspaces for their school communities. Makerspaces are never done. GREAT makerspaces are always growing, evolving, and shape-shifting, and by nature are agile and responsive. So even if you are an educator who already has a makerspace, it is my hope that this book will help ensure that your makerspace is one that is most effective and meaningful for your school community.

At the core of this book is the belief that

> **No two makerspaces should be exactly alike, because no two school communities are exactly alike.**

Whether readers are creating a makerspace for a classroom, library, or another space within a school, this book will help them uncover and roll out a space that is vibrant and meaningful to their school now but also sustainable into the future.

It is my hope that readers of this book will have already read my first book, *Worlds of Making: Best Practices for Establishing a Makerspace for Your School*, which articulated the underlying pedagogy and philosophy and provided a foundation, rooted in research and best practices, for makerspaces in K–12. This *Kickstart Guide* builds on the research presented in *Worlds of Making* and showcases those practices by highlighting key components of planning and creating a makerspace and leading readers through the process of doing so. Perhaps the most rewarding part of writing this book for me was having the

opportunity to showcase GREAT makerspaces around the world, including in Ghana, Mongolia, Australia, and America.

All makerspaces have the capacity to be great. This book is filled with step-by-step, practical ideas and will help readers shape their space to create a unique learning environment that their students need, want, deserve, and value. While anyone can go out and buy a bunch of "stuff," those who dedicate the time and effort to the process outlined in this book will create spaces that are meaningful to their school communities. The book is also filled with examples of GREAT makerspaces across the world. It is my hope that highlighting the work of others will help you learn and grow from the work of your peers.

Please write in this book. It is intended to inspire you to make and create. I encourage you to write, brainstorm, doodle, sketch, create, and MAKE in the book itself. Look at this book as a blank canvas that has unlimited possibilities and is just waiting for you to make your mark. I believe passionately that teachers who model making will build better makerspaces.

This book contains

 Step-by-step guidance for planning a **GREAT** makerspace

 Explanations of the process of planning and creating a makerspace, demystifying and breaking down barriers to innovation

 Lots of activities and strategies to try

 Plenty of room for brainstorming your ideas

 A framework for purchasing items for your makerspace

 Support for setting up your physical makerspace

 Ideas and inspiration for turning your makerspace into a unique learning environment that your students need, want, deserve, and value

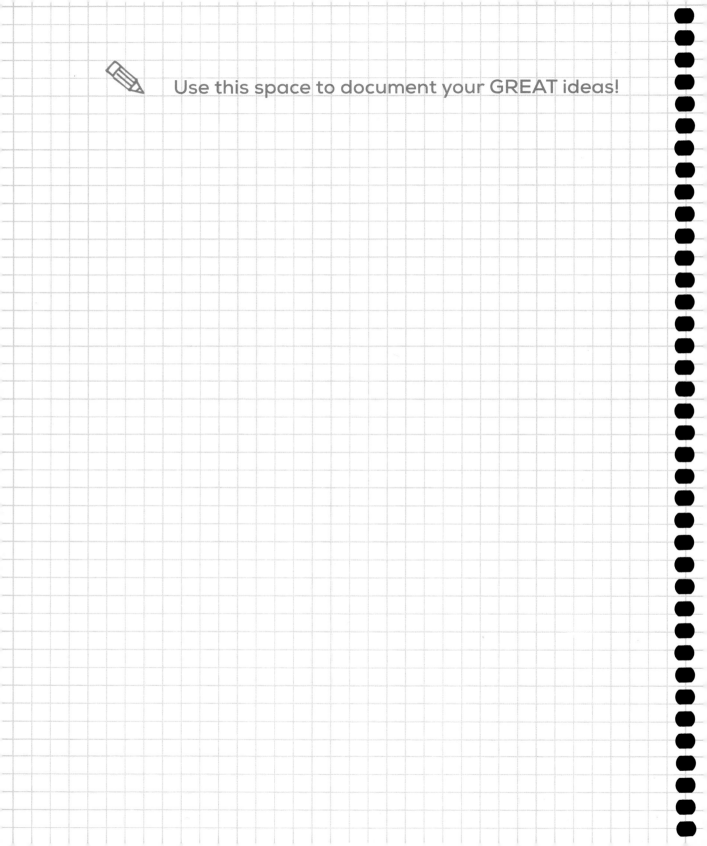

Use this space to document your GREAT ideas!

Photo courtesy of Jackie Child

Photo courtesy of Kellyanne Burbage

Photo courtesy of Kerry Cowell

Photo courtesy of Kerry Cowell

Photo courtesy of Kerry Cowell

Personalized
Deep
Empowering
Equitable
Differentiated
Intentional
Inspiring

1 THE SEVEN ATTRIBUTES OF A GREAT MAKERSPACE

THE SEVEN ATTRIBUTES OF A GREAT MAKERSPACE

My work with schools across the nation on planning and creating makerspaces has proven to me that while anyone can create a makerspace, there are distinct differences between makerspaces and GREAT makerspaces. Makerspaces touch the surface of impacting student learning, whereas GREAT makerspaces allow students the opportunity to take a deeper dive into their learning. The students who have visited my makerspace most regularly have been the students who are most disaffected by traditional schooling. At the most fundamental level, our makerspace has allowed them to find their passion and foster a love for learning. This naturally has helped them focus on other areas, too, leading to higher achievement in their content-area classes. All students who visit our makerspace benefit from intrinsic motivation and self-directed learning. GREAT makerspaces make learning fun and motivate students to learn. The skills the students gain extend their learning into the real world and provide them with benefits that reach well beyond their schooling.

GREAT makerspaces are unique to your school community and not only vibrant now but also sustainable into the future. All too often, schools go out and buy the "stuff"—the things that other schools with makerspaces have bought, or things that are trendy and schools feel they should buy. What usually happens in those instances is that the space is exciting for a short period of time but, ultimately, that excitement fades. GREAT makerspaces plan for the future and understand that a makerspace is never done. It is always evolving and growing and taking shape.

The seven attributes of a GREAT makerspace serve as a guide for school districts and educators as they plan makerspaces for their school communities. Makerspaces should be **personalized** to your school community, promote **deep** understanding of concepts, provide **access** to all students to ensure equity, invite **student-driven** exploration, **differentiate** for students' needs, convey an **intentional** vision, and **inspire** students to make.

Let's explore what each of these components looks like in GREAT makerspaces.

Photo courtesy of Gina Seymour

Photo courtesy of Gina Seymour

Personalized

A thematic approach to planning your makerspace ensures that you uncover themes that are unique, relevant, and meaningful to your school community.

GREAT makerspaces are personalized and uncover themes that are unique, relevant, and meaningful to your school community. Take, for example, New York high school librarian Gina Seymour, who has adopted the theme of "compassionate making" in her makerspace at Islip High School, in Long Island, New York, which allows her students the opportunity to explore societal themes such as compassion, empathy, and social action through the creation of authentic content and products. Students who want to make a difference in her community visit her MakerCare station to create authentic contents and products. She emphasizes that high-tech makerspaces are not necessary in a school, that all you need to support themes are inexpensive supplies along with children who wish to take action in their community through engaged self-expression.

Another example of a school makerspace with themes that are unique, relevant, and meaningful to a school community is the makerspace at Belgrave Heights Christian School in Melbourne, Australia. Their makerspace, the DC (Discovery Centre), is a place where the school community can gather to imagine, create, explore, invent, tinker, and make. In addition to the themes of construction, engineering, and geography, they also have adopted the theme of faith. This theme allows for student devotion time wrapped around making and exploration.

Deep

Be sure to provide opportunities for your students to take their learning deeper.

Makerspaces in and of themselves do not necessarily promote deeper learning. Does your makerspace have depth? GREAT makerspaces provide opportunities for students to take their learning deeper. For example, many makerspaces have Legos. Legos are all about themes such as engineering, design, and architecture. For those students who enjoy designing with Legos, it is critical to find additional ways to support the themes behind Legos. Students who enjoy Legos should have other opportunities to experience engineering, architecture, and design, and not just be limited to one activity. This affords them rich experiences and innovative ways to take their learning deeper than if their experience began and ended with Legos.

Photo by Dorie Glynn at Kirk Elementary School in Cypress-Fairbanks ISD

Samantha Edwards, library media specialist at Fogelsville Elementary School, has created many opportunities for her students to take their learning deeper. Using Schoology, she created a competency-based learning model in her Media Center for her fifth graders. Students master the curriculum while also obtaining open-ended exploration and increased time in their library makerspace. As students master concepts, they are awarded online badges. After three to four units are mastered each quarter, students receive open-ended exploration time at the Innovation Station of their choice in their makerspace. Samantha also has tried

to create a print-rich environment conducive to researching robotics, engineering, circuitry, design, and bookmaking, among many other topics, and has supported her students' interests in the Innovation Stations she developed. Providing students with the innovative tools to explore, integrating the curricular topics from their classroom experiences, and making books and digital resources available to them is the best way she has found to ensure her students are more invested in the learning opportunities she provides in her Media Center.

Samantha tries to foster a mastery of the four Cs—creativity, collaboration, communication, and critical thinking—in all the activities she has in her makerspace. These include the following:

Photo courtesy of Kellyanne Burbage

- **Research Lego design project:** Students researched famous buildings as a curriculum integration project in their Media Center. After they completed their research using the print-rich environment and digital resources, they taught the class all about their famous building. Students then used the green screen, as well as movie-making software from the makerspace, to complete their presentation to the class. They also had a choice to use either the Legos in the makerspace to build their famous architectural building/landmark or the 3-D printer to design and create a replica. Having the innovative makerspace tools, as well as the print-rich and digital resources, has allowed for her students to extend their learning beyond the surface to a deeper level.

- **Lego storytelling:** Students created designs using the Legos in the makerspace and were tasked with locating a book from their library to help tell their "story." For example, if they created a Lego design that had a horse in it, they needed to locate a book about horses to gather some facts to include in their story. They also were able to use digital resources when looking for supporting information.

- **Collaborative experience with fourth-grade space exploration project using the green screen and movie-making software:** After teaching a unit on the research process, fourth-grade students were assigned the task of choosing a planet and researching it. Their challenge was to create an alien from that planet. Students captured pictures of their alien in front of the green screen. Then students used an app to manipulate their alien's mouth so it looked like it was talking. The alien shared five key points about its planet via video recording. Since the original photo of the alien was captured in front of a green screen, a space scene could be added by the students during editing. To support the students beyond the tools for this project, Samantha displayed space exploration and alien books, and encouraged students to use their digital resources for further exploration.

- **Wonder Foxes – robotics team and K'NEX team:** With several after-school clubs that meet and compete, students are able to extend their makerspace skills beyond the classroom walls. These competitions provide an in-depth exploration of robotics, engineering, mathematics, and much more.

Photo courtesy of Medfield Public Schools, Massachusetts

Empowering

The setup of your physical makerspace, along with the items in it, should invite *all* students in.

Makerspaces have the potential to empower students in endless ways. GREAT makerspaces ensure that everything created is celebrated by showcasing student creations both within the school community and with an authentic audience. In my makerspace, I take photos of all student creations and hang them up in a gallery that not only celebrates what our students have done but also serves as inspiration for their peers to make and create, too. In addition, I share their creations on Instagram and Twitter, using the hashtag of our makerspace, #worldsofmaking.

Jennie Martin, K–5 STEAM teacher for the Keystone Oaks School District, showcases group projects that students have done in her makerspace, since those are hard to split up and take home. She also uses her space to showcase the work of students who are easily frustrated and need some encouragement.

GREAT makerspaces can be deeply empowering to students on a very personal level. Take, for example, Michael, who started high school with no friends and as a result was oftentimes dejected and despondent. Michael began coming to our makerspace and became our computer science star. He decided to use his skills to create an arcade system. Yes, he created this arcade system because he had a passion for computer coding, but his real reason for creating the system was to use the skills he knew he was strong in to create something other kids would enjoy playing, which would hopefully make them want to be his friend. This is, in fact, what occurred. Now Michael continues to visit our makerspace and has a network of peers who accept and appreciate him.

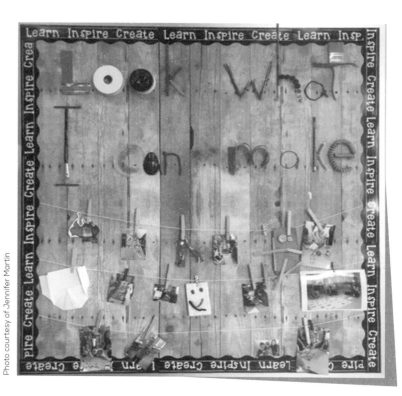

Photo courtesy of Jennifer Martin

GREAT makerspaces give students a choice and allow them to take control of their own learning. They also help students feel more socially included by fostering peer-to-peer relationships and building creative confidence. Makerspaces offering open access to materials, supplies, and easy-to-start activities will guarantee successful and independent learners while limiting frustration.

The setup of your physical makerspace can play a significant role in empowering students. The use of visual cues can communicate and give necessary directions. This strategy can be especially beneficial for learners who have difficulty following complicated directions or remembering instructions for extended periods of time.

Having a low barrier of entry into makerspace activities will ensure that any of your students—regardless of their academic proficiency or even whether English is their primary language—can begin making with very little or no

teacher facilitation. My school district has 42 home languages; therefore, we have a high number of students who are English-language learners. These students, who are often limited during school by their level of English proficiency, are able to flourish in our space and grow in language development because of the hands-on experiences they have in an authentic setting. There are days we have our engineering students sitting right alongside our English-language learners, all working together and learning from each other.

Our makerspace provides equal access to learning. Students who have unique learning needs thrive in our space because it allows them to express themselves without fear of failure. For example, one of my students is Ethan, a young man who has been diagnosed on the autism spectrum and therefore has unique learning needs. As you can imagine, Ethan has faced many challenges during his schooling, both social and academic, which oftentimes have left him feeling frustrated and with a negative view of school. Despite his feelings about school, Ethan began to visit our makerspace during his lunch period two years ago. Since then, not a school day has gone by that he has not visited our space during his

Photo courtesy of Laura Fleming

lunchtime. He is fully engaged in making and creating from the moment he enters the space until the moment he leaves it. He has managed to work on projects that involve concepts even I knew nothing about. As a result, he has had the opportunity to rise to a leadership role in our space, some days teaching me about what he is doing, other days teaching his peers. He also helps monitor the day-to-day activities and has helped streamline the workflow in our makerspace, making him a true leader. As a result of his amazing accomplishments in our space, his performance in his academic classes has also improved and he has also developed many friendships. Ethan now likes to come to school and has stated that he wants to go to college for electrical engineering, based on the skills he has gained in our makerspace.

The setup of your physical makerspace, along with the items in it, should invite *all* students in, therefore engaging them and empowering them. It is possible to have a makerspace that challenges students without just making things harder than usual. Rigor does not necessarily equal difficulty. Despite this low barrier of entry, it's also possible to ensure that students find challenges here, with the opportunity to take their learning as far as they choose—a student-driven learning environment. GREAT makerspaces are inclusive, meeting the needs of *all* learners, and help build learner independence.

Photo courtesy of Walhallab, Netherlands.
Photo credit: Thomas Boelaars, Thomas Boelaars Creative

Equitable

Create an inclusive learning environment that encourages tinkering, play, and open-ended exploration for *all*.

GREAT makerspaces are equitable. They democratize learning by making materials, supplies, and concepts available and accessible to *all* learners. By properly planning your makerspace, you can build an environment that provides equity of opportunity, as well as one that levels the academic playing field for your students.

One important attribute of an inclusive makerspace is that it encourages tinkering, play, and open-ended exploration for everyone. GREAT makerspaces are not open and available to just an elite portion of the student body, nor are they just a reward for students who are high achievers or behave well. The students who visit our makerspace most frequently are those who might otherwise never have earned the chance to do so. These are the same students who have gone on to do and make the most amazing things in our space. Take, for example, Brian. Brian was disengaged, uninterested, and withdrawn at school. He put forth no effort in his regular classes and therefore was not performing well. On his own time, Brian began visiting our makerspace. It was clear from the beginning that Brian got a lot of enjoyment out of working with his hands in the authentic ways our makerspace offered him. He began visiting our makerspace's Take Apart Tech Station on a daily basis. He became so interested in what he was doing in our space that he started to show up to school early and stay late. He took apart so many computers that he eventually challenged himself to put them back together so they worked again, sometimes even using a cardboard box as a case.

Photo courtesy of Laura Fleming

Other children became curious about Brian's work, and he began developing friendships. Those friendships led him and his peers to form a team in which each student had a role in the process of taking apart and reassembling the technology. Finally, the students realized that they had a story to tell. These students, who all refused to read and write in their classrooms, started blogging about their experiences. At first they were concerned that their lack of writing skills would keep them from being able to accomplish this. I emphasized to them that many would benefit from reading about their experiences and that they simply should not let anything stand in their way. So they went home and filled their nights and weekends with writing about their journey. They worked together as a team in developing the blog, with some of the students recruited by their peers to be the writers, others the editors, and others the photographers. The teachers of these students began seeing a change in each student's affect. The love for learning that they experienced in our makerspace went with them back into their

classrooms, and their teachers not only found ways to integrate the work these students were doing into their classes, but they discovered that these students, who were once the most disengaged, were now the most engaged.

Making curricular connections in your makerspace can serve as a powerful means of building equity into your makerspace. Pay special attention to the classes offered in your school, as well as clubs and extracurricular activities. Pull out concepts that are frequently taught or available to a select number of students and make them available and accessible in your makerspace to anyone who has an interest. For example, in my school, an engineering class is taught in my building; however, only one engineering class is available and most of the students who enroll in that class are boys. I decided to include engineering concepts in my makerspace, borrowing from what was happening in the engineering class but making those things accessible to all students.

GREAT makerspaces democratize learning, but the question is:

> **How do we ultimately reach all learners?**

Equity and access are at the heart of ensuring that all students have the opportunities available to them that school makerspaces present. Makerspaces should be designed for the highest amount of accessibility, taking into consideration the practice of universal design in education.

Increasing student access to making related materials can broaden physical makerspaces and help reach more of our learners. Just as students no longer need to be tied to a computer lab, making doesn't have to be confined to the makerspace. Mobile makerspaces can liberate learners from the limitations of a physical makerspace. By transcending the traditional makerspace, students don't have to come to a makerspace; you can take your makerspace to the students.

Several years ago, Principal Brad Gustafson and the Greenwood Elementary team collaborated on a new way to deliver hands-on and cutting-edge learning experiences to students. They invested in a fleet of kid-friendly carts that can be checked out like library books. The carts contain high-tech, low-tech, and no-tech tools recommended by students and staff. Today, their mobile makerspace fleet is capable of transforming any classroom or hallway into a space where students and staff are empowered to engineer, experiment, and fail forward.

By mobilizing their makerspaces, they paved the way to an ethos of innovation as opposed to a single "destination space" reserved for innovative thinking. Brad believes that by putting cutting-edge tools into the hands of students who might not otherwise have the opportunity to engineer (or kids who might not naturally gravitate to science and math learning tools), his team is breaking down barriers and empowering a new generation of learners. It's a matter of equity. He emphatically shares that all students deserve the opportunity to collaborate, create, and invent their future.

Brad has shared countless examples of the culture-spreading power of a mobile strategy. He's also seeing teachers create "pop-up" makerspaces in their classrooms. Another benefit of mobile makerspaces is the ability to collaborate with other schools by sharing resources (e.g., ideas, supplies, and carts) at half the cost. When "making" becomes part of a classroom, school, and district culture, all students win, regardless of what classes they take or who their teacher is.

Brad provokes the question, "If students are living in a connected world (and I think they are), why would we limit their learning based on bricks, mortar, and artificial boundaries?"

GREAT MAKERSPACES DEMOCRATIZE LEARNING

Perhaps the most powerful attribute of a GREAT makerspace is that it democratizes learning. Makerspaces allow you to democratize learning by making materials, supplies, concepts, and resources available and accessible to all students, regardless of their proficiency level, social status, or even level of language development. On a daily basis, I have seen our makerspace successfully demonstrate this.

Photo courtesy of Kellyanne Burbage

HOW WILL YOU ENSURE THAT YOU REACH ALL YOUR LEARNERS?

 BRAINSTORM YOUR IDEAS HERE:

 THE KICKSTART GUIDE TO MAKING GREAT MAKERSPACES

Differentiated

Provide materials, activities, and supplies that meet the needs of *all* students. Create a learning environment that nurtures a community of learners.

All GREAT makerspaces are differentiated and effectively meet the needs of mixed-ability learners. Makerspaces can differentiate based on materials, content, learning environment, and process. A suite of multimodal materials is essential in meeting a wide variety of student learning needs and engagement styles. An easy way to differentiate access to content in your makerspace is to build in student choice. Centers or workstations in a makerspace can be used to encourage students to collaborate with their peers and can be a means of supporting differentiation. Consider the idea of alternative seating. In my makerspace, we have a combination of active seating for those students who need to move around, spaces to stand, high-top tables for students to sit or stand, and low stools and a countertop for those who prefer that setup. The unique learning environment of a makerspace invites students of varying abilities to work together. Creating a community of learners will make all students feel welcomed in your space.

A differentiated makerspace can allow students of all abilities to participate, experience success, and ultimately flourish. Students need to be supported as they develop increasingly sophisticated ideas over time. What this means for each student is different. In our makerspace, our students' first interactions are often just about discovering. Gradually, through skill building, collaboration, and critical

Photo courtesy of Medfield Public Schools, Massachusetts

thinking, our students progress to much more complex processes related to engineering and scientific inquiry.

Many schools have begun using a specific process for making and creating in their makerspaces, such as design thinking, but it is important that the process is differentiated and eventually student-driven. Initially, process can be differentiated in many ways, including by providing varying levels of support for a task in a makerspace. As learners become more comfortable, we can gradually release the responsibility of a structured making process to complete learner independence. This type of flexible, self-directed learning will empower as well as enhance all learners' unique learning abilities.

To help students uncover and articulate the process they used to make and create, they can reflect on the various iterations involved in their making.

Ask them questions such as these:

- **What did you make/do?**
- **What did you do first, second, and so on?**
- **What materials did you use/work with?**
- **What surprised you during the process?**
- **What frustrations did you experience, and what did you do about them?**
- **What steps did you use this time that you might want to use again?**
- **What steps do you think you want to try next time you make something?**

Students can also interview their peers or maker mentors to refine their own making process. The guiding question during these interviews should be: "Where do I see this maker doing something that I can do in my own making process?" You can support this by teaching students how to ask good questions, having students reflect on their own making, and finding a place in their own making where they can use what they learned from a maker mentor.

Intentional

Have a vision for your makerspace.

One of my favorite books is *Start With Why*, by Simon Sinek. In that book, he talks about the importance of knowing your *why*: the purpose, cause, or belief that inspires you to do what you do. Ask yourself, *why* do you want a makerspace and what will the purpose of the space be? It is important to be able to discover your own unique *why* and to articulate that vision in the form of a mission statement. GREAT makerspaces have a vision that drives their space. Having a clear intention for your makerspace is so important; Part 2 of this book is entirely devoted to helping you craft yours!

Photo by Dorie Glynn at Kirk Elementary School in Cypress-Fairbanks ISD

Inspiring

Create the conditions to inspire your students to *want* to make.

A question I am frequently asked by schools that have makerspaces is: *How can we get more of our students engaged in our makerspaces?* Many educators feel that their direct instruction is what is needed to engage students in making experiences. While I do believe that there can be a place for some instruction for skill building in a makerspace, I don't believe it is the only strategy that should be used for engaging our students; nor is teacher-led instruction the only way we can encourage our students to be creative or innovative. Rather than forcing students to make, GREAT makerspaces create the conditions to inspire our students to *want* to make.

In my makerspace, I work hard behind the scenes to create a learning environment that inspires our students to want to make. For example, hanging on the walls of our makerspace, we have copies of real patents for many items that are familiar to our students, such as smartphones, video-game controllers, Legos, and cars. We have issues of *Make: Magazine* strewn all over our makerspace and a list of 100 makerspace ideas created by Canadian educator Ian Cunliffe. We also have photos hanging throughout our library of our students' maker creations. These photos are a great way to celebrate our students' accomplishments, but they also serve as inspiration and oftentimes motivate their peers to make, too.

Our makerspace in the New Milford High School library.

Photo courtesy of Laura Fleming

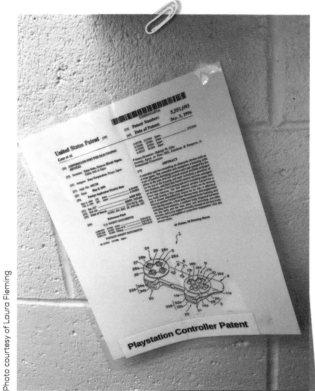

A Playstation Controller Patent hangs on the wall of our makerspace.

How Do You Rank the Attributes of a GREAT Makerspace?

Rank the seven attributes of a GREAT makerspace from the most important to the least important, based on what you and your team want to implement in your school community.

Provide ideas or questions you have about implementing them.

Please note: You don't have to implement all seven attributes to create a GREAT makerspace. You can ease into it. Makerspaces are always evolving and growing over time.

Rank	Attribute	Ideas	Questions
	Personalized		
	Deep		
	Empowering		
	Equitable		
	Differentiated		
	Intentional		
	Inspiring		

I imagine . . .

Use this space to document your GREAT ideas!

Photo courtesy of Kelsey Ray

Photo courtesy of Kelsey Ray

Photo courtesy of Laura McDonnel

Photo courtesy of Jen Holberg

Photo courtesy of Jackie Child

Reflect on your own school experiences, gather your team, and brainstorm your vision for your makerspace. How can making transform school for your students?

MAKING GREAT MAKERSPACES

MAKING GREAT MAKERSPACES

Teaching is a reflective practice. To create a GREAT makerspace for your learners, you first have to see the world through a child's eyes. Spend some time reflecting on your own schooling experiences. This will help you gain an even deeper understanding of what education is and what it should look like, and what role your makerspace will play.

Reflect . . .

Which of these words describe your own education experiences as a student?

Circle or highlight the words that stand out to you—or add your own!

		Add your own!
Lackluster	Lonely	_____
Empowering	Engaging	_____
Exciting	Dull	_____
Linear	Stimulating	_____
Traditional	Memorable	_____

What was one of the most memorable learning experiences you had as a student in a classroom?

What was one of the least effective learning experiences you had as a student in a classroom?

What was one of the most memorable learning experiences you had outside of a classroom?

What was one of the least memorable learning experiences you had outside of a classroom?

ON THIS MAKER JOURNEY, YOU ARE BOTH A TEACHER AND A STUDENT

Challenge: Imagine that you could design the perfect makerspace for your childhood self. What would you have loved to see in that makerspace? What experiences or materials would have allowed you to explore your dreams and ideas?

_____

_____

_____

_____

_____

_____

_____

_____

_____

_____

_____

_____

_____

_____

_____

GET IN TOUCH WITH YOUR INNER MAKER!

Making can be anything. If you could make anything, what would you make? There are no wrong answers here. Your answers can be tangible things or not. Get creative! Nothing is off limits! This exercise is about digging deep and starting to get to know yourself as a maker.

Sketch it out here!

 Stop! Don't go any further until you try this same exercise with your students. Ask **THEM** what **THEY** want to make! Use the next page to brainstorm with your class.

IF YOU COULD MAKE ANYTHING, WHAT WOULD YOU MAKE?

I would make _____.

I would make _____.

I would make _____.

I would make _____.

I would make _____.

I would make _____.

I would make _____.

I would make _____.

I would make _____.

I would make _____.

I would make _____.

I would make _____.

I would make _____.

I would make _____.

MAKE

MAKE

MAKE

MAKE

A **makerspace** is a metaphor for a

unique learning environment that

encourages tinkering, play, and

open-ended exploration for **all**.

What Does Making Mean to You?

Making is a deeply personal thing to those who experience it. I define a makerspace as a unique learning environment that encourages tinkering, play, and open-ended exploration for *all*. Most students view it as an opportunity for their individualism to shine. We as educators cannot possibly try to define making as one thing or try to define what it means for our students. The educational makerspace is based on student ownership of what making and learning means to them. When asked, my own students have said the following:

Making is the reason for being alive.

Making means to make things that make the world a better place.

As a girl, making means that you can show that you can do stuff, too.

Making means that you have a mind of your own.

Making means making things, making art.

Making is something you are proud of.

Making means doing something that you have never done before.

Making is putting your own story into what you make.

Making means that I can show my ideas and do whatever I want with them.

Making is a way to be creative and have fun at the same time.

Making means building things that you find important.

Making is creating something that shows who you are.

Making lets us express ourselves and be creative.

WHAT DOES
MAKING MEAN TO YOU?

_____

_____

_____

_____

_____

_____

_____

_____

_____

_____

_____

_____

_____

_____

_____

_____

_____

Build Your Team

The most successful school makerspaces I have seen are the ones that have been planned using a team approach. Teams can consist of school leaders, members of educational foundations, parents, teachers, students, public librarians, members of the community, or local businesses. Really, anyone can be a part of your team!

There is no set number of people that need to be on a makerspace planning team, and it is certainly something that can be done by an individual. But when representatives from the broader school community are involved, they will feel invested in the space, and you will be likely to receive more support. Involving key stakeholders in your space can lead to amazing opportunities for collaboration, community involvement, and support. Once a team is in place, it is my recommendation that you continue the rest of the planning outlined in this book with them. In my experience, the more time and effort put into properly planning a makerspace, the more successful, vibrant, and meaningful the space will be.

Many schools have included students on the committees for planning their spaces. The more involved students are in the process of creating the space, the more ownership they will take over the space, and this will just make them feel all the more empowered and help turn the space into the student-driven space you want it to be.

Planning your makerspace alone? No problem! There are many opportunities during the makerspace planning process to include students, colleagues, and community members.

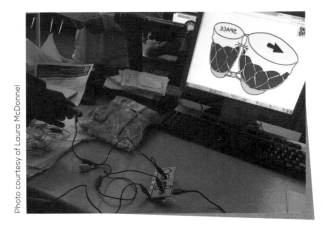

Photo courtesy of Laura McDonnel

	Who will be on your team?	What will their role be?

Find Makerspace Inspiration

After you have your team in place, it's time to hit the road! Schedule site visits to other schools that have makerspaces. If you are not sure who does, put a shout out on social media for schools in your surrounding area that have makerspaces. On Twitter, Instagram, and Facebook, be sure to use the hashtags #makingGREATmakerspaces, #makerspace, #makered, and #worldsofmaking in your inquiries. Also check your surrounding communities for makerspaces that are in the towns or museums. All types of makerspaces are worth visiting. For example, I've been inspire by co-op workspaces, children's museums, and even Disney World! Each of these inspiring spaces provided me with unique ideas that I was able to bring back and apply to our makerspace. Take lots of photos of anything and everything that inspires you in those spaces, even if you don't quite know what they mean yet!

Use the space below to reflect on your visits. Use the next page to showcase the photos that inspired you. Can't get out for visits? Try surfing the web! Take a look at images of makerspaces on Pinterest or Instagram, and save those that grab your attention. Or do both!

Space Visited	Takeaways From the Visit

MAKE A LIST

OF THE MAKERSPACE RESOURCES YOU FIND ONLINE FOR REFERENCE WHILE YOU'RE PLANNING

_____

_____

_____

_____

_____

_____

_____

_____

_____

_____

_____

_____

_____

_____

PRINT OUT PHOTOS

OF MAKERSPACES OR MAKERSPACE ELEMENTS YOU HAVE FOUND INSPIRING, AND REFLECT ON THEM HERE

I felt inspired by this photo because

_____

_____

_____

_____

_____

What jumps out at me in this photo is

_____

_____

_____

_____

_____

What I especially like about this photo is

_____

_____

_____

_____

_____

I felt inspired by this photo because

_____

_____

_____

_____

_____

What jumps out at me in this photo is

_____

_____

_____

_____

_____

What I especially like about this photo is

_____

_____

_____

_____

_____

Why Do You Want a Makerspace?

Hopefully, after reading my first book, *Worlds of Making: Best Practices for Establishing a Makerspace for Your School*, you have a good understanding of the value of makerspaces and how they can complement curriculum and instruction. Before you can begin to plan a makerspace, it is important to build on that foundation and ask yourself: *Why* do I want a makerspace?

Are you just interested in starting a makerspace because it is a trend or a buzzword you have heard?

Are you interested in starting a makerspace because it is something you see other people doing and you feel like you should be doing it, too?

There needs to be more to it than that—because your purpose for planning a makerspace will strongly influence the quality of the makerspace.

It is important to be able to discover the purpose of your makerspace.

Photo courtesy of Walhallab, Netherlands. Photo credit: Thomas Boelaars, Thomas Boelaars Creative

THINK...

Why do you want a
makerspace?

_____

_____

_____

_____

_____

_____

_____

_____

_____

_____

_____

_____

Articulate Your Vision

Once you discover the purpose for your makerspace, it is important to articulate that vision and write it down in the form of a vision statement. All GREAT makerspaces have a vision.

What is it you are trying to create?

What is it you are trying to do?

This statement will help you make meaningful decisions as you plan and create your own unique spaces. Your vision statement will help you convey to others what your makerspace is trying to achieve and will help people better understand your space.

I suggest that you do the next few exercises together with your makerspace team. If you're doing it on your own, ask a mentor or colleague what they think about certain ideas. You might also form a student focus group to get their opinion on the makerspace vision.

A good place to start this process is to think about your school's mission/vision statement and then think through how your makerspace can be seen as a physical representation and embodiment of that strategy. The vision of the makerspace should closely align with the vision of the school or district.

Your makerspace can be a physical representation of your school's mission statement.

When we planned and created our makerspace, we used our district's mission statement to help shape the unique learning environment we were trying to build. As a result, our school's makerspace is a physical manifestation of our school's mission statement.

Pulling directly from my school's mission statement, I aimed to create a unique learning environment that reflected this mission.

District's Mission

NEW MILFORD PUBLIC SCHOOL DISTRICT MISSION

The New Milford Public School District provides relevant, innovative and rigorous educational opportunities to students at all grade levels.

The District is resolute in its attention to the development of the whole child by providing a comprehensive range of experiences essential to building capacity for independent and responsible living.

The program is designed to prepare all students to meet or exceed NJCCCS, think critically, master the challenges of life-long academic, cultural, social, economic, emotional and professional advancement, as well as constructive participation as citizens in an interdependent global society.

The District embraces family and community as active partners in a unified effort to develop students into self-directed, self-confident adults on their journeys to becoming the next generations of entrepreneurs, builders, artists, designers, inventors, scientists, educators, caregivers, protectors, workers and leaders.

Our Makerspace Vision Statement

WELCOME TO
WORLDS OF MAKING
@NMHS

· WHAT IS WORLDS OF MAKING @ NMHS?

WELL, THAT IS UP TO YOU, THE MAKER!

THE SPACE, BOTH PHYSICAL AND VIRTUAL, IS A PLACE FOR YOU TO COLLABORATE, HACK, INVENT, SHARE, CREATE, MAKE AND DO.

YOU HAVE BEEN GIVEN THE TOOLS YOU NEED TO GET STARTED.

WHERE IT GOES IS UP TO YOU.

THE WORLD IS YOUR PLATFORM

#WORLDSOFMAKING

In the Bronxville Union Free School District, they created their maker-space vision statement based on the Bronxville Promise, a framework of four dispositions: innovation, leadership, critical thinking, and engaged citizens. These four dispositions are designed to guide the way students plan their course of study, the way teachers organize teaching and learning activities, and the way parents and the larger community support the school.

The Promise	Makerspace Vision Statement
To innovate, discover, and create To make something new from what you know To find your voice and communicate clearly, in order to lead with passion and persistence To think critically, explore nature, history, and culture To gain the understanding and courage to change To collaborate and serve To engage in the world around you and make it a better place	 Photo courtesy of Laura Fleming

WHAT IS YOUR SCHOOL'S MISSION STATEMENT?

_____

_____

_____

_____

_____

_____

_____

WHAT PIECES FROM YOUR SCHOOL'S MISSION STATEMENT COULD BE RELEVANT TO YOUR MAKERSPACE?

_____

_____

_____

_____

_____

_____

_____

_____

Ideally, your vision statement should be

- a succinct statement about what your makerspace is trying to achieve, to help parents, administrators, fellow staff members, community members, and the students better understand your space, and

- a memorable and inspirational summary that describes the reason for your makerspace existing—one that will help motivate students and even continue to attract others to the space.

It is important to note that makerspace vision statements are unique to their school communities and represent a vision that is sacred to them. When developing your vision, do not copy another school's vision. Craft a statement that is as unique to your school community as the space you are working to create.

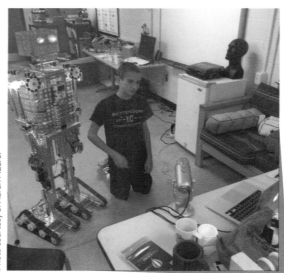

Photo courtesy of Aaron Maurer

EXAMPLE VISION STATEMENTS

READ through the sample makerspace vision statements on the next few pages.

CREATE a list of what you feel are defining characteristics of a makerspace vision statement. What do these vision statements have in common? What elements stand out to you? What do you want to make sure to include in your own vision?

1. _____
2. _____
3. _____
4. _____
5. _____
6. _____
7. _____
8. _____
9. _____
10. _____

PLAN how you aspire to use a makerspace vision statement in the future. What role can it play in your makerspace?

For example, you might reference the vision statement in makerspace planning meetings, make a poster to hang in the space, send it home in a letter to families—anything! How will you use your vision statement?

_____

_____

_____

We are the STEAMmakers. We explore Science, Technology, Engineering, Arts, Math, and Making. We are about tinkering, wondering, exploring, inventing, rethinking, designing, creating, problem solving, collaborating, brainstorming, and innovating.

We hang out in the design loop and ride it 'round and 'round, and we know that our thinking gets better when we try many iterations and rely on the power of teamwork. We know that together we excel, and by connecting with others through the power of the internet we are unstoppable.

We are interested in almost everything: robotics, engineering, virtual and augmented reality, 3-D design, electronics and circuitry, video creation, building, deconstructing, drones, life science, earth science, physical science, coding and programming, design challenges, gaming, and creating art . . . whatever that may be.

We get amazed by simple science like the magic of a drop of water, yet also crave advanced technology like programming Raspberry Pi and Arduino computers. We craft beauty from duct tape and program robots to follow complex code. We design catapults to study physics and we make stop-motion videos. We make prototypes from cardboard and from 3-D printers, and sometimes we make things that fail. Then, we make improvements and we learn.

We are the STEAMmakers. We are the curious ones. We are the future.

BUILDING COLLABORATIVE CURIOSITY TO EMPOWER RICH LEARNING EXPERIENCES. PUSHING BOUNDARIES SO WE DREAM BIG. INSPIRING OTHERS TO IMAGINE, DESIGN, CREATE, AND INNOVATE WHAT LEARNING CAN REALLY LOOK LIKE.

Our Makerspace Is...

A place where everyone's talents are celebrated and where everyone's passions come to life (whether they know it is a passion or not!).

A place where everyone can find and meet challenges at their own level, and collaborate with their peers to find solutions.

A place where students can learn to become leaders; sharing and teaching their craft(s) to others.

TIPS FOR DEVELOPING A VISION STATEMENT FOR YOUR MAKERSPACE

Keep it short!

Vision statements should be short—two or three sentences at an absolute maximum. (It's fine to expand on your vision statement with more detail elsewhere, but think of your vision statement as an elevator pitch for your makerspace.)

Keep it unique!

The statement should be specific to your makerspace and describe a unique outcome that only you can provide. Generic vision statements that could apply to any makerspace won't cut it!

Keep it simple!

The statement should be simple enough for educators and community members to understand.

Make it ambitious enough to be exciting but not so ambitious that it seems intimidating or unachievable.

Statements should also align with and support the district/school mission to ensure that the makerspace is a part of the district culture.

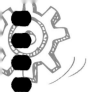

WHAT IS YOUR VISION FOR YOUR MAKERSPACE?

Brainstorm your first draft here. You can always go back and edit this statement as your space evolves.

_____

_____

_____

_____

_____

_____

_____

_____

_____

_____

_____

_____

_____

_____

From Vision → Call to Action!

Once you have your vision statement written, it is time to write this vision in kid-friendly words to display in your makerspace. Displaying your vision statement in "kid-speak" can not only make your space pop, but it can also inspire your learners to visit the space. Even just a few simple words can serve as a call to action. These words will convey to your students that you have created a space for them, and just by reading your "kid-speak" vision statement, they will know the purpose of your space right away. We can see an example of this in Kevin Jarrett's space during his time at Northfield Community Middle School in New Jersey:

Photo courtesy of Kevin Jarrett

And another example can be found in Texas educator Krissy Venosdale's inspiring space:

Photo courtesy of Krissy Venosdale

An easy way to transform your makerspace vision statement to kid-speak is to pull out just the action verbs.

The Oxford Hills Technical School in Maine has a series of project-friendly workspaces scattered around their school community. The large words hung in the spaces represent their DECA theme. DECA is a career and technical student organization for marketing, hospitality, and finance students. The smaller words serve to inspire students to make and create.

Photo courtesy of Wendy Robichaud, EdD

Photo courtesy of Wendy Robichaud, EdD

Photos courtesy of Wendy Robichaud, EdD

Wisconsin fifth-grade teacher Matthew A. Wigdahl used Dan Pink's framework for motivation as the inspiration for his classroom's makerspace vision. He posted three categories/phases of student work:

Autonomy: I can do this correctly, safely, and independently. (Students are practicing the tools and testing to earn a badge for proficiency with the physical or digital tool.)

Mastery: I can show that I understand this information. (Students read and rehearse science/other content and pass a quiz to demonstrate understanding and earn a badge.)

Purpose: I can use the tools *and* my knowledge to solve a problem and make something useful. (Students combine the first two phases into a project of their choosing—and they employ design thinking to give structure to the process.)

Photo courtesy of Matthew Wigdahl

 Tip: An easy way to turn your makerspace vision statement into kid-speak is to circle all the action verbs.

WRITE YOUR VISION STATEMENT IN KID-SPEAK BELOW:

_____

_____

_____

_____

SKETCH YOUR IDEAS FOR DISPLAYING THESE WORDS IN YOUR MAKERSPACE:

I imagine . . .

Use this space to document your GREAT ideas!

Photo courtesy of Barbara Lee

Photo courtesy of Catherine Barrett

Photo courtesy of Barbara Lee

Photo courtesy of Jen Holberg

Photo courtesy of Catherine Barrett

The Makerspace Planning Process
Understand
Assess
Consider
Develop
Order

3 NO COOKIE-CUTTER MAKERSPACES ALLOWED!

THE MAKERSPACE PLANNING PROCESS

Parts 1 and 2 of this book were meant to help you better understand the attributes of a GREAT makerspace and help you craft a vision for your space. At this point, I hope you are feeling inspired by other makerspaces you have seen. Now it is time to get down to some serious planning for your makerspace.

In my book *Worlds of Making: Best Practices for Establishing a Makerspace for Your School*, I pointed out the importance of properly planning and creating a makerspace. I always explain to schools that I wish I had made the planning process diagram a full-size color poster that readers could tear out of the book to hang on their wall. That is how important the planning process is in creating a GREAT makerspace. So now, in this new book, there is a full-size poster for you to hang and use as a visual tool for planning your makerspace. Allow the maker education community to learn from you! Take a photo of your poster and share on Twitter or Instagram, using the hashtag #makingGREATmakerspaces.

As I lead you through the process for planning and creating your makerspace in the next part of this book, feel free to plan and create your space in real time, right along with me, using your poster or the "Makerspace Action Plan" on the following pages, so that at the end you have a real plan for creating your space and can hit the ground running!

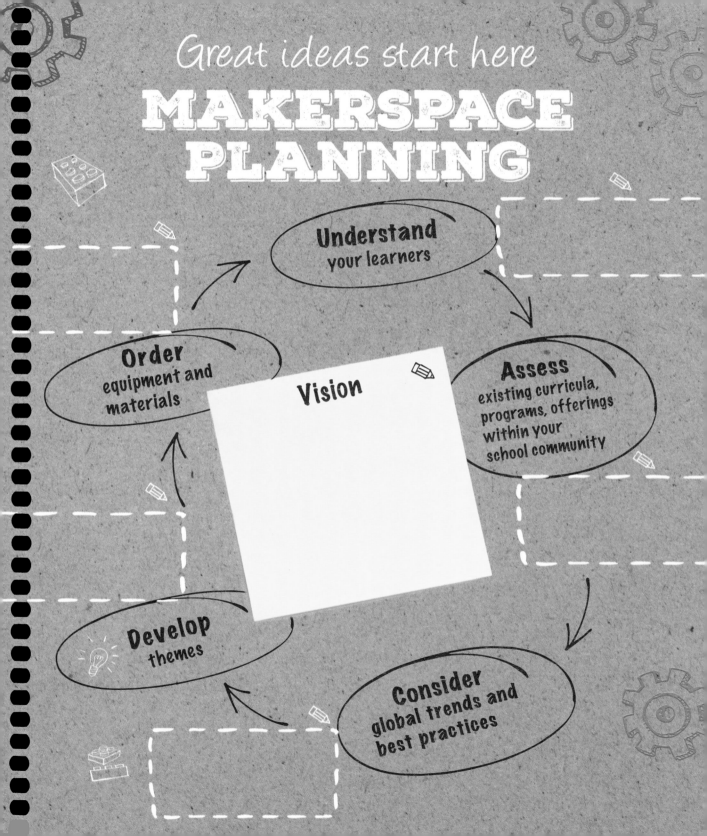

Great ideas start here

MAKERSPACE PLANNING

Understand your learners

Order equipment and materials

Vision

Assess existing curricula, programs, offerings within your school community

Develop themes

Consider global trends and best practices

Makerspace Action Plan

Actions	Who Will Be Responsible?

Resources Needed	Target Date for Completion

Planning Process

Gather your team! It is time to move on to planning your makerspace.

At the heart of this process is student voice and taking the time to understand your learners. That is the first step. From there, it moves on to assessing curricula, programs, and offerings within your school community. This phase of the plan-

Photo courtesy of Barbara Lee

ning process allows connections to be made to standards, if that is what your team chooses to do. The next phase of the makerspace planning process is to consider global trends and best practices, linking your makerspace to what is happening in the wider world.

The makerspace planning process is data-driven. It is up to you and your team to work hard at gathering raw data from the first three phases of the planning process to help you as you move on to the fourth. The fourth phase of the planning process is about using those data you collected to develop themes for your makerspace. Being able to back makerspace decisions with data is something that many of the educators I have worked with have found useful in justifying the decisions they make. The final phase of the planning process is about supporting those themes with appropriate and meaningful materials, supplies, and resources.

Educators often use a resource-driven approach when planning a makerspace, making it all about the stuff. I believe in taking a thematic approach. Anyone can buy a bunch of stuff and put it in a corner, and yes, that stuff is alluring and fun for a bit. But that excitement usually fades, and schools are left wondering why. More often than not, this happens because no thought went into planning the makerspace beyond what to buy. A thematic approach to planning your makerspace is beneficial because it

- offers a personalized approach for planning your makerspace,
- streamlines the ordering process by giving you a much more targeted lens,
- provides opportunities for your students to take their learning deeper, and
- ensures that you have a suite of multimodal materials to meet the varying learning styles of the students who will be visiting your space.

It is important to remember, too, that along with the data you collect from this makerspace planning process, you have developed a makerspace vision statement that should drive your thinking, planning, and decision making.

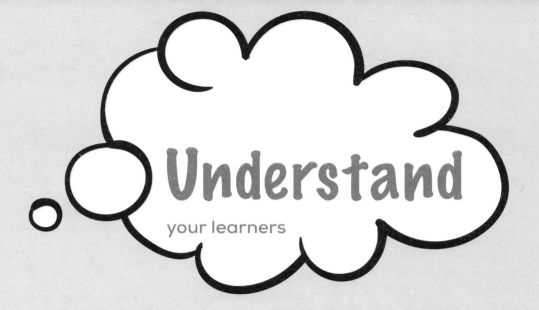

Understand
your learners

All GREAT makerspaces connect to their students. The first phase of the Worlds of Making makerspace planning process is to **understand your learners**. No planning should happen without first starting with your learners.

It is possible that at this point, your students do not even know what a makerspace is. That's okay! It is still possible for you and your team to take the time to find out what your students want to do. By doing so, not only will you guarantee that the space includes things students are interested in doing or want to know more about, but you will help them feel like they had a hand in planning your space. This will make them feel more empowered and ensure that your space is the student-centered, student-driven space it should be.

> **What are their passions?**
>
> **What are the things they wish they had time to do in school?**
>
> **What do they do outside of school?**
>
> **Interests? Hobbies? Extracurricular activities?**

The goal of this phase of the planning process is to find out what the needs, wants, and interests of your students are, both in school and out of school. Find out what kinds of things they do outside of school and what kinds of things they want to do in school. Discover what kinds of hobbies or extracurricular activities they engage in or want to engage in. Without the voice of the learners, makerspaces are nothing more than a bunch of stuff in a room.

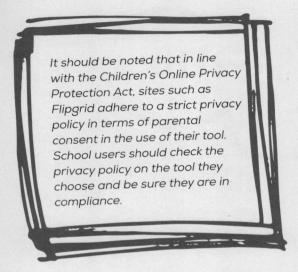

It should be noted that in line with the Children's Online Privacy Protection Act, sites such as Flipgrid adhere to a strict privacy policy in terms of parental consent in the use of their tool. School users should check the privacy policy on the tool they choose and be sure they are in compliance.

How you and your team collect these data is entirely up to you. The idea is to do it in a way that works best for your school community. Perhaps you want to administer a formal survey to the entire student body or a segment of the population via a Google form or another type of online form. Perhaps you want to have students themselves design the survey and administer it to their peers. Perhaps you want to do something a bit more informal and give a traditional paper-and-pencil questionnaire, such as the one I have included for you in this book. For the youngest of learners, you might want to interview them, or they could use an online tool such as Flipgrid, which will allow them to speak their answers and allow you to easily collect and curate them.

However you choose to complete this phase of the makerspace planning process is perfectly acceptable. The idea at this stage is to collect the raw data and hold on to those data for later use. This student feedback will play a very important role in the development of themes for your makerspace.

Photo courtesy of Hein Bruijnesteijn

Take a look at this phase of the makerspace planning process in action in the work of Dr. Kristine Malik, resource center director at Notre Dame Academy in Toledo, Ohio. After taking my online course, Creating Spaces for Students to Make, Kristine started off the planning of her makerspace with the assessment of student needs. She documented this process on her blog, where she indicated that she chose to survey 10% of all grade levels at her school (Grades 7–12). She wrote survey questions with the goal of assessing the need for a makerspace. Her survey was administered using a Google form, with all randomly selected participants taking the survey in a designated space at a designated time.

The following is an excerpt from Kristine's blog (NDASRCmakeover.blogspot.com).

By Dr. Kristine Malik

I printed out the student answers for each survey question. I kept the answers for each question separate. Then I separated each answer by cutting them apart into strips. Then I started to "code" them. Coding means that I assigned a word to summarize what the answer is about. The image below shows the strips of paper. Most has the letter "I" in front of it to mean that these strips describe "Inventing."

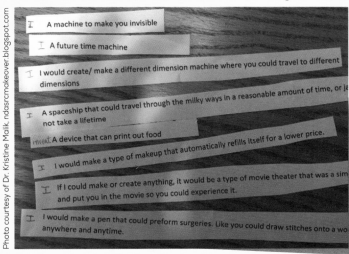

Photo courtesy of Dr. Kristine Malik, ndasrcmakeover.blogspot.com

This continuous process of coding, data interpretation, and exploration led to the emergence of categories, patterns, and themes.

This is very useful because knowing your data inside and out leads to the ability to organize it in a way that it becomes **compact and cohesive**.

I used the following iterative process for coding the data for all the questions:

The answers for each of the survey questions were sorted into groups or categories based on their similarities. For instance, I received these interesting answers to the *"If you could make/create anything, what would it be?"* question:

- Make a time machine
- Create a teleportation device
- Invent a way to pause time

You have to give credit to these students to think outside the box or should I say: to think like there is no box!

But what to do with these answers? Well, I created a larger category I called "Futuristic Ideas" and put them all in there!

After sorting the other responses the following larger categories emerged:

- Invent (57% of participants said this)
- Art (13%)
- Make world a better place (8%)
- Crafts (6%)

The largest category, "Invent" contained the following descriptions as to what the students would like to invent:

- Things to improve daily life (26%)
- Cure diseases (11.5%)
- Futuristic ideas (11.5%)

The "Things to improve daily life" contained examples such as invent a phone battery that lasts weeks; create makeup products; make computers work faster; create bigger school lockers; and create fun apps.

Discussion of Results

Dream Big	Learn to Do	Create at School	Opportunities to Have
Invent	New skill	Invent/build	Resources for learning
Art	Career/life skill	Cope with anxiety	Socialize more
Service	Foreign language	More service	Career help
Crafts	Technology skill	Games	Foreign language
			More service

Courtesy of Dr. Kristine Malik, ndasrcmakeover.blogspot.com

The columns of Dream big, Learn to do, Create at school, and Opportunities to have are the final categories that emerged after the coding process.

Color-coding is a very helpful part of the data analysis process:

- The red boxes indicate tech learning/inventing/building.
- The yellow boxes are for any activity that leads to some form of relaxation and stress relief.
- The gray boxes indicate a desire for foreign language learning.
- The green boxes refer to students wanting to engage in more Christian service opportunities (which is useful feedback for the school's Pastoral Service Office).
- The blue boxes indicate career help (which is relevant for the school's career and guidance counseling department).
- The purple box indicates that the students would like to have more resources for learning, specifically resources for academic writing and research purposes.

Here is the final table that helped me make the selection for the maker-space stations.

Themes in NDA Makerspace

Arts/Crafts	Invent/Build/New skill learning	Games/Less stress
Jewelry making	App development	Card games
Calligraphy	Video editing	Board games
Coloring	Website creation	Trivia games
Baking	Coding	Peer listener
Knitting	Making robots	Wall to write feelings
	3-D models	Quiet place to go when stressed
	Build Lego	More bonding across grade level
	Cure disease	
	Make daily life easier	
	Makeup product	
	Foreign language	

Some of these could be flexible stations: to be rotated in and out

23

Source: Courtesy of Dr. Kristine Malik, ndasrcmakeover.blogspot.com

To help you get started, on the next page is a student survey template that you're welcome to reproduce and use!

STUDENT SURVEY

What are your hobbies?

What do you enjoy doing in school?

What do you want to learn how to do?

What do you wish you could do or make in school?

If you could make anything, what would it be?

What kinds of clubs or activities are you in?

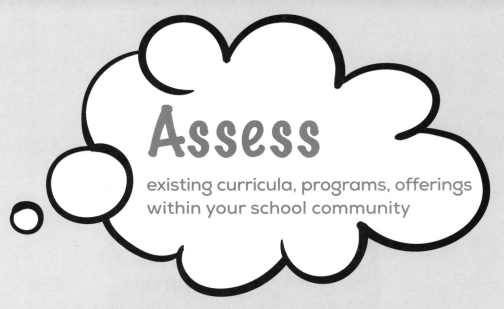

Assess

existing curricula, programs, offerings within your school community

The second phase of the Worlds of Making makerspace planning process is to **assess existing curricula, programs, and offerings within your school community**.

To collect data from this phase of the planning process, you can pull from a wide variety of sources. As a school librarian, something I found to be the most effective when planning my space was talking to classroom teachers about how my makerspace could connect to what they were doing in their classrooms. Oftentimes classroom teachers have great ideas for ways your makerspace can complement, enrich, or extend their curricular demands. It is also wise to read through curricula yourself to find opportunities for your makerspace. The idea is for you to gain a good understanding of what is happening in your school or classroom and what is not. That "what is not" might present the greatest opportunities for your makerspace. Talk to colleagues across your personalized learning network about the things happening in their schools, and see if you can discover some new and exciting things to include in your makerspace. On the next page is a fantastic example from Long Branch New Jersey Public Schools for how to effectively integrate English language arts curricula into making.

Photo courtesy of Barbara Lee

Another thing to consider during this phase of the planning process is the data-driven needs of the school community. These data-driven needs can be a result of assessments that reveal particular skills the makerspace can target or support. Florida library media specialist Elizabeth Zdrodowski adjusted her makerspace to support the literacy needs of her students by including more literacy activities

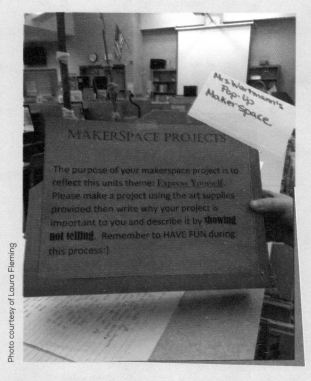

MAKERSPACE PROJECTS

The purpose of your makerspace project is to reflect this units theme: Express Yourself. Please make a project using the art supplies provided then write why your project is important to you and describe it by **showing not telling**. Remember to HAVE FUN during this process:}

Mrs.Wortmann's Pop-Up MakerSpace

Photo courtesy of Laura Fleming

in their makerspace. For example, during National Poetry Month, they had two poetry stations where students authored original poems using preprinted words that were in envelopes marked according to parts of speech. If a student needed a word they couldn't find, Elizabeth would quickly create it and add it to the collection. They also had two stations set up for blackout poetry. Students really loved this activity, especially when they realized they could create visual art along with their original poem. They also have used Bamboo Pads and Animation-ish to design animated vocabulary words, created trailers for classic literature such as *Hamlet*, and used origami to create shapes representative of a book.

This is also the phase of the planning process in which you can connect your makerspace to any set of relevant standards you choose. GREAT makerspaces connect to their school communities, curricula, and standards. Gather the raw data from this phase of the planning process and save it for when you begin to develop the themes for your makerspace. For example, in my book *Worlds of Making: Best Practices for Establishing a Makerspace for Your School*, I suggested ways to connect your space to the Common Core, the ISTE Standards, or the AASL Standards. It is also a good idea to consider state and technology standards, as well as Next Generation Science Standards. Doing so allows you to make direct curricular connections to what is happening in your school. It also allows you to effectively address standards while creating an informal, student-driven space. **Connecting to standards does not have to be limited to classrooms.** K–12 makerspaces are unique learning environments that can support the learning outlined in any set of standards. Standards serve as a framework for deeper learning.

Connections to the standards in my makerspace have led to many exciting collaborations with classroom teachers. The world history students at my school embarked on a maker journey related to their content area and shared their maker stories through a video reflection. The goal in creating this unit was to offer a new lens for opening up to students the content and related standards that needed to be covered. This unit was a collaboration between me, the library media specialist at my school, and our world history teacher.

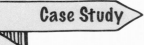

Unit Title: Engineering an Enduring Understanding

Desired Results

Ultimately, we wanted to be sure that the unit understandings were "enduring"—that the deeper understanding of the content the students gained had enduring value beyond the classroom. We strove to create a framework that would ensure their learning would be meaningful and valuable outside of school. We accomplished this by offering them opportunities for authentic, discipline-based work while giving them license to be creative. This unit pulls principles from project-based learning, inquiry-based learning, and maker education. We chose to connect this unit to the Renaissance because it is such a creative period in history and would speak to our students' creativity.

Learning Plan

- Hook and engage students in the content.
- Link student "making" to the unit's enduring understandings and student-generated essential questions.
- Through the making process, give students opportunities to rethink and revise their work, or iterative process.

(Continued)

(Continued)

- Through a video reflection, give students the opportunity to exhibit their understandings and deeper inquiry.

- Use materials and supplies and tech to provide an authentic, hands-on experience for the student.

- Foster collaboration, communication, problem-solving, and teamwork.

Assessment Evidence

We provided multiple opportunities within the unit for students to demonstrate mastery of the unit learning goals through varied and frequent formative assessments. We made the decision from the start *not* to evaluate *what* the students made, or *how* they made it. We encouraged them to take risks and fail and fully supported the iterative process. The video reflection was used as a tool to ensure that student learning became an enduring understanding, and it served as our summative assessment. Through our guidance, students created videos that were thoughtful and meaningful and that linked directly to our unit. Students were able to show, through their video reflections, how they gained a deeper understanding of the Renaissance through making.

Process

Day 1 kicked off with immersing the students in the Renaissance through group research and collaboration. We had a mini-lesson about using our school databases as resources, and using Chromebooks and their own devices, students crafted paragraphs in a Google doc that reflected their basic understanding of the Renaissance. This served as our first formative assessment.

Day 2 kicked off with a mini-lesson on crafting essential questions. Our world history teacher introduced our students to the work of Grant Wiggins and Jay McTighe. We spoke to students about what an essential question is and gave them guidance for crafting their own essential questions in relation to the Renaissance. We encouraged students to tap into their passions in creating their essential questions and choose areas of the Renaissance that would allow them to further explore their passions and interests. We explained to them that their essential question would drive their maker journey.

On Day 3, we had a group discussion about the challenges in creating essential questions. Many students expressed that they had to revise their questions several times before getting them just right. This opened up a discussion on the importance of having a growth mindset. We empowered them to take risks and chances in this unit and explained the process and strategies of the iterative process. We reminded them that their classroom was a judgment-free zone and that they should feel free to explore whatever spoke to them. The creation of their essential questions served as another formative assessment.

From here, students began collaborating with their groups on choosing what they wanted to make to help them demonstrate deeper learning about their essential question, and therefore an enduring understanding of the Renaissance. We spoke to them about connecting what they decided to make to their passions and how this relevance was going to make what they learned about the Renaissance have value and meaning beyond just the classroom or this unit, a true enduring understanding. Through their essential questions, many students chose to compare elements of the Renaissance to things in the modern world, helping them uncover that much more relevance.

Students then began brainstorming, designing, and planning the creation of their final authentic products. They were encouraged by us to be open-minded, follow their passions, be creative, and have fun. Students were captured and enthusiastic about being able to take control of their learning and create and discover things that had meaning to them, especially in regard to a topic they felt often did not have relevance to them. The things the students decided to make and do were nothing short of amazing. Some of their creations included fashion design and 3-D art representations.

The unit concluded with students creating a 1-minute video that reflected their group's process of creation, essential question, and enduring understanding of the Renaissance.

Photo courtesy of Laura Fleming

Hair and makeup of the Renaissance and how it influenced modern trends

What role can the standards play in your makerspace?

How do you unpack standards to inform your makerspace planning?

How can you address standards in your makerspace?

Sometimes educators are hesitant to incorporate close curricular ties in their makerspace because they are afraid it will limit creativity, but it is possible to connect your makerspace to standards without losing the essence of what GREAT makerspaces should be. Opportunities in your makerspace for students to invent, tinker, create, make, and do can allow students to develop skills and demonstrate learning outcomes addressed in standards. An easy way to make those connections is by using I-H-R.

- **I = Identify:** Identify the standards you want to make connections to.

- **H = Highlight:**

  ○ Highlight the nouns, *what* the student should know—the topics. This declarative knowledge will help you determine the concepts you want your students to retain.

  ○ Highlight the verbs/verb phrases, *what* the student should be able to know—the skills. This procedural knowledge will help you determine what processes your students need to demonstrate to meet their learning goals.

- **R = Redefine:** Rewrite the standard using student-friendly language.

Use the framework on the next page to help you and your team unpack standards to make connections to your makerspace.

After completing I-H-R for identified standards:

- Integrate the topics into makerspace themes during the fourth phase of the makerspace planning process.

- Include skill-building activities related to the skills.

- Post rewritten kid-friendly standards in the makerspace to inspire and motivate, communicate learning intentions, and indicate success criteria in your makerspace.

MAKING CONNECTIONS IN YOUR MAKERSPACE USING I - H - R

I = IDENTIFY   H = HIGHLIGHT   R = REDEFINE

Identify Standard

Highlight
NOUNS/Topics

Highlight VERBS/
Verb Phrases/Skills

REDEFINE Standard Using
Student-Friendly Language

Assess
existing curricula,
programs, offerings
within your school
community

Needs of Teachers

Concepts Taught in School

Gaps Your Makerspace Can Fill

Key Concepts Related to Standards

Consider

global trends and best practices

The third phase of the Worlds of Making makerspace planning process is to **consider global trends and best practices**.

What is happening in the world?

This is such a significant component of planning a makerspace yet oftentimes is the most overlooked. This phase of the planning process will help ensure that what is happening in your makerspace connects meaningfully to what is happening in the world. These connections will help your makerspace feel relevant to your students and the world they live in. The data you gather from this phase is important and will help you craft authentic learning experiences for your students that in turn have real-world applications.

To gather the information you need, analyze important topics or trends, both inside education and outside the education sphere. By doing so, you will create engaging makerspace experiences that matter to your students and will endure beyond just your makerspace, and even beyond the four walls of your school.

Begin by researching trends in education and evaluating what types of experiences your students would benefit from exposure to. For example, virtual reality is a current popular trend. Would your students benefit from or enjoy having virtual reality experiences in your makerspace? You can also create context and meaning in your makerspace by making connections to news headlines and events. For example, for a long time we couldn't turn on the news or read a newspaper without hearing or reading about drones. Would it be valuable to integrate drones into your makerspace? What about the idea of connecting your makerspace to pop culture and related people, topics, and themes?

Canadian teacher librarian Diana Maliszewski's makerspace has taken on the theme of clothing. This theme ties to the real-world issues and topics of social justice and eco-literacy, because students are reusing, upcycling, and repurposing clothes. Not pushing her students in any particular direction, what she saw was students making a lot of things to wear. This helped shape their group inquiry question—"How might clothing reflect our identity?"—which they then spent time exploring. This included watching the video "The Secret Lives of Our Clothes" by Greennovate and on-site trips to thrift stores to learn how they reuse and recycle clothes, as well as to purchase clothes for their projects.

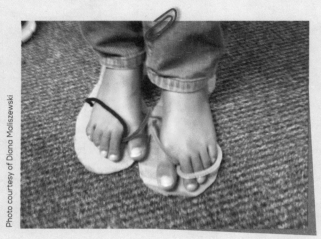

Photo courtesy of Diana Maliszewski

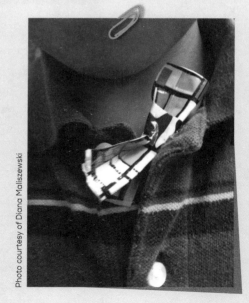

Photo courtesy of Diana Maliszewski

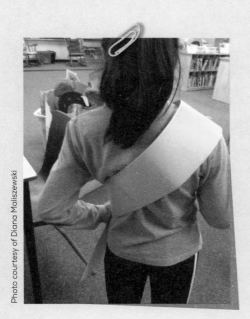

This phase of the makerspace planning process has led me to develop our most innovative makerspace themes, such as molecular gastronomy, wearable technology, and machine learning. Validating things in our makerspace that typically fall outside of the realm of school led to increased student engagement and allowed students to explore whatever aspects of those themes appealed to them most. Hold on to the raw data you collect from this phase to be used in the next phase of the planning process.

CONSIDER
GLOBAL TRENDS
AND BEST PRACTICES

CONNECT YOUR MAKERSPACE
TO THE WIDER WORLD

Trends in Education

Trends Outside of Education

Newsworthy Items

Develop
themes

The fourth phase of the Worlds of Making makerspace planning process is to **develop themes**. Now is the time to analyze and evaluate all the data you collected from the first three phases of the planning process.

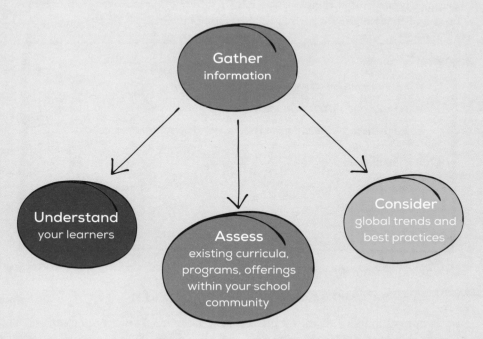

Gather
information

Understand
your learners

Assess
existing curricula,
programs, offerings
within your school
community

Consider
global trends and
best practices

You are then going to synthesize those data to develop themes for your makerspace.

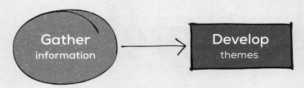

Although this is a themed approach to planning a school makerspace, you should not feel limited by the themes you choose or by a particular number of themes. Students should not be required to limit their making to just the themes you have in place or to the themes that are in your comfort zone. Sometimes their making takes them in directions you just cannot predict. Makerspaces should encourage students to make, and that making should have no limits or ceiling. In addition, you do not need to have activities for every one of your themes happening all at the same time. You certainly can rotate themes in and out of your makerspace on a schedule that works best for you and your students. Some schools highlight a theme per month in their makerspace. In my makerspace, we have some themes that happen all the time, for example, 3-D printing and design. We have other themes that rotate in and out of our space on an irregular basis and that I highlight for a special activity or event.

What a theme *is*:

- **A launchpad to kickstart making and creativity**
- **Inspiration for students, to spark ideas**
- **Help for those who might have trouble working with zero guidelines**

What a theme is *not*:

- **A rule**
- **A restriction**
- **A ceiling**

Creating Themes

- Look at all your ideas/findings and find similar concepts.

- Begin grouping those things into categories/themes. It is helpful to create groups of keywords that have characteristics in common. For example, keywords such as *drones* or *paper airplanes* can be placed in a group centered on the theme of flight.

Tip: Organize all your findings into categories. To do this, analyze your data to find similar concepts and begin grouping them into categories (themes). You might want to do this on a whiteboard, use a digital graphic organizing tool of some kind, or even just use sticky notes. Write each idea on a sticky note, color-code them, and sort them by moving them around until categories and themes start to emerge.

Photo courtesy of ©iStockphoto.com/olaser

Photo courtesy of ©iStockphoto.com/livgeorge

The development of themes for your makerspace could be the most challenging part of the planning process, especially when you have a wide variety of random ideas, thoughts, and feedback, but it is especially important because it ensures that you begin to uncover a makerspace that is unique to your school community. It is important to note, too, that you do not need to have a certain number of themes. The themes you develop will be based on the data you collected; therefore, the types of themes, as well as the number of themes you end up with, will be unique.

My makerspace themes have included robotics, flight, hacking/remixing the Web, molecular gastronomy, and electricity. Some of these themes were developed based on student interests, some were based on concepts that were not offered at my school as any part of any class, and others were based on global trends that I felt our students would benefit from having some exposure to. My themes are unique to my school and my students and my space, and they might not be relevant to your school, your students, or your space. I have worked with schools who developed themes such as service (doing good for their community), whimsy (which included many artistic activities), health and wellness (to counteract the stress and pressure of their STEM-focused high school), and shopping (which included real-world math practice through stores built by children in their makerspace).

Photo courtesy of Catherine Barrett

While, yes, we tend to see things that are common in makerspaces, such as 3-D printing and design, there really are no wrong answers when it comes to developing your themes. Many people associate makerspaces with STEM-related concepts, but themes don't have to be limited to those. The idea is to create themes that are based on the information you collected from the first three phases of the planning process, ensuring that they connect with your learners, as well as your school community and the wider world. I encourage you to think outside the box and feel confident and secure in any theme choices you might make.

Library and instructional technology specialist Jonathan Werner crafted a detailed plan for the launch of their makerspace at Cape Elizabeth Middle School. In that plan, he highlighted their planned makerspace themes, which include the following:

- Robotics
- Programming
- Construction
- Electronics
- Games
- Claymation
- Recycled and Upcycled Art
- Gardening and Growing
- BreakerSpace

- 3-D Printing and Design
- Wire and Metal Craft/Jewelry
- PaperSpace
- Book Art/Printing/Publishing/ Bookbinding/Block Printing
- Movie Making
- Fabric and Yarn Arts
- Inspiration Station

High school library media specialist Michelle Shaw's makerspace themes include the following:

- Bridge Design
- Extreme Mazes and Dot-to-Dots
- Circuits
- 3-D Printing and Design
- Sewing
- Solar Panels
- Coding

The Islip High School library has a makerspace centered on the themes of Hispanic heritage, propulsion, holidays, sports, seasons, music, and "for the birds." The creator of this makerspace, librarian Gina Seymour, believes that makerspaces can support societal themes such as compassion, empathy, and social justice through the creation of authentic content and products. She emphasizes that there is no need for a high-tech makerspace in your school and that all you need to support themes such as these are inexpensive supplies and children/teens who wish to take action in their community through engaged self-expression. Rather than centering makerspaces on kits or items, GREAT makerspaces focus on the themes and skills those things support.

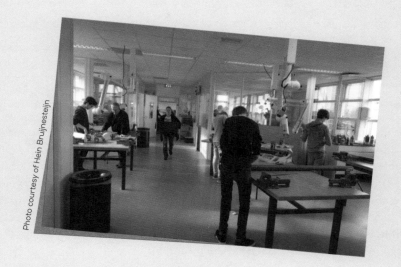

Photo courtesy of Hein Bruijnesteijn

POSSIBLE MAKERSPACE THEMES

_____   _____

_____   _____

_____   _____

_____   _____

_____   _____

_____   _____

_____   _____

_____   _____

_____   _____

_____   _____

_____   _____

Congratulations! With your themes in place, you are well on your way to making a GREAT makerspace. One of the keys to ensuring that your makerspace is sustainable into the future is to revisit the makerspace planning process each school year. This will help you determine if your themes are still relevant to your school community. We have dropped themes in our makerspace because they are no longer relevant to our space. We also have put themes on the back burner to revisit in the future. We also have adopted new themes based on the new data I collected by revisiting the makerspace planning process.

Please note: The final phase of the makerspace planning process is to order equipment, materials, and supplies. This phase is so important that I have dedicated the next section of the book to it!

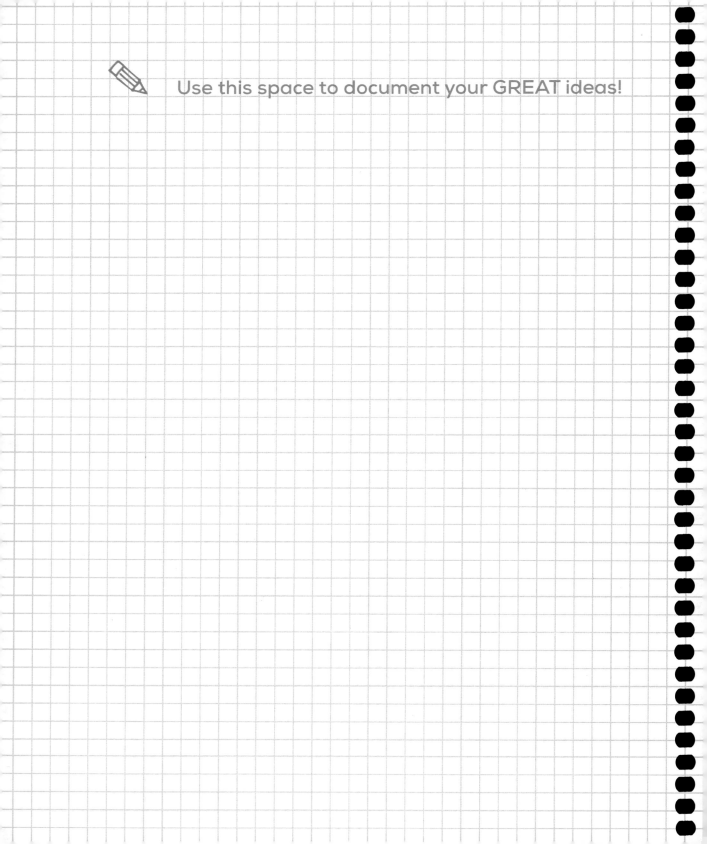

Use this space to document your GREAT ideas!

Photo courtesy of Catherine Barrett

Photo courtesy of Diana Maliszewski

Photo courtesy of Diana Maliszewski

Photo courtesy of Diana Maliszewski

Photo courtesy of Mongol Makers NGO, Mongolia

Based on the themes you uncovered in the makerspace planning process, you will stock your makerspace with the materials, resources, and supplies your space needs!

4 GET THE MOST BANG FOR YOUR BUCK!

Order
equipment and materials

The fifth phase of the Worlds of Making makerspace planning process is to **order equipment and materials**. I have dedicated an entire section of this book to this phase of the planning process since it is the one educators have the most questions about.

If you have ever wondered the following, then you are not alone!

 What is popular and used in other makerspaces that I should buy?

How can I ensure that what I buy will give me the best bang for my buck?

Anyone can go out and buy a bunch of stuff, and while that stuff might be fun for a short amount of time, frequently, the excitement fades and schools are left wondering why. In many cases, these schools began their makerspace planning with this phase of the planning process. Since my goal is for you to create not just a makerspace but a GREAT makerspace, purchasing materials and supplies is the *last* phase of the Worlds of Making makerspace planning process.

Budgeting

GREAT makerspaces are possible on *any* budget. Sometimes your best supplies and resources are right there in your library, school, or community already.

Sometimes they come from a dollar store, and other times, if your budget allows, they might be more expensive or big-ticket items. It's about making the most of what you have available to you.

Once you have your makerspace themes in place, deciding what to stock your makerspace with will be that much easier. If you are lucky enough to have a budget for your makerspace, search the Internet for resources, materials, and supplies related to your themes. This approach streamlines the ordering process and gives you that much more of a targeted lens. Be sure to check discount or dollar stores, too! I have seen many GREAT makerspaces built on a very limited budget.

No-Cost Resources

✓ **Crowdfunding campaigns:** Projects can be funded through parents, community members, or the general public. Some popular crowdfunding websites are DonorsChoose, GoFundMe, and Kickstarter. *Be sure to check your individual school district's policy on crowdfunding campaigns.*

✓ **Grants:** I recommend that schools interested in grants check with their state's Department of Education for grant resources and information.

✓ **Donations:** Donations can serve as a great opportunity to introduce your space to parents and community members. Share with them your vision statement, as well as your makerspace themes, and ask them to donate items they feel would help support your space. *Be sure to check your individual school district's policy on donations.*

✓ **Your own school:** Trawl your school to see what resources you can gather and repurpose. If you have the space, consider creating a maker closet filled with supplies for your students and teachers to access.

✓ **Digital resources:** Consider creating a digital extension to your makerspace by curating websites related to its themes. This is a free way to support your makerspace while also adding to the mobility of your space and increasing access to it. A site such as Symbaloo can be an effective tool for organizing the websites related to your themes, or you can make pertinent links available using an online tool such as Diigo or even keep it as simple as listing websites in a shared Google doc.

✓ **Recycled items:** A free and fantastic way to encourage children to think creatively and problem-solve with open-ended exploration in your makerspace is to give them access to recycled materials. Fill your makerspace with materials children can use to design and create their own projects and inventions.

Photo courtesy of the Public Library of Mount Vernon and Knox County, Ohio

✓ **Your school or public library:** Search your school's library collection for books related to your makerspace themes. Pull those books, or ask your librarian to pull them, and create a special display in your school's library or even right in your makerspace. Contact the public library and alert them of your maker-space themes. Ask them to create a special display of books related to your themes so you can encourage your students to visit the public library. Check out the makerspace theme on the left for Teen Librarian Toolbox's summer reading challenge!

✓ **Open educational resources (OER):** Resources that reside in the public domain are no-cost teaching and learning materials available online for anyone to use, modify, or share with others. For example, visit OER Commons (oercommons.org), search for your makerspace themes, and see what is available for you to use.

✓ **People:** Parents, community members, local businesses, and beyond can be an effective means of supporting your makerspace themes. Alert community members of your themes and ask them to donate their time and energy to your makerspace efforts. Oftentimes parents and community members will have hobbies or professions related to the themes in your makerspaces and will be willing to visit your space to demonstrate their skills or talk to your students about what they do.

BYOT (Bring Your Own Toolbox)

The current generation of students has grown up with technology and uses it in every aspect of daily life, and for many this will include the jobs they pursue. Equipping students with the skills they need in life outside of school and beyond the makerspace is a powerful component of the maker movement. An often overlooked but necessary skill set for those students who will be pursuing careers related to the themes in your makerspace, such as electricity, engineering, and design, is leveraging advancements made in digital tools available on their personal devices.

As a librarian in a BYOD (bring your own device) high school, in addition to providing opportunities for my students to use their mobile devices as creation tools, I also promote the idea of using their personal devices as toolboxes. As a result, in our makerspace we have a BYOT (bring your own toolbox) initiative. This initiative was spurred by a conversation with our school electrician, who was doing work in our library and instead of using physical tools was using tools on his smartphone. He emphasized how important devices have become for those in skilled trades.

The experiential learning opportunities offered in makerspaces are some of the most valuable tools we have to prepare students for the workforce they will be entering. We as maker educators need to create new ways of learning to help build a better workforce. **Stocking your makerspace with tools and supplies can be very beneficial, but for our students, their most powerful tool might be right in their pockets!**

> If your students do not bring their own devices to school, many of these apps can be installed on tablets in your makerspace, giving your students a similar experience.

Please hang the next page in your makerspace to help kick off your BYOT initiative!

MAKERSPACE APPS

You are welcome to use any tools in our makerspace that you need; however, the most powerful tool you have could be right in your pocket! Download the following FREE apps on your personal device to create your own digital portable toolbox!

- **iHandy Level:** A great tool to level any flat surface

- **i-Ruler:** Supports both inches and centimeters and is capable of measuring things much longer than a phone

- **Plumb Bob 5th:** A 3-D measurement tool that helps you check vertical or horizontal alignment or measure a distance or an angle; helps you verify the verticality of lines or walls

- **Pocket Protractor:** A measurement tool for your device that will help measure any angle; just put an object on the screen and move the red line, and it will follow your finger

- **Photo Measures Lite:** Easily share and save measures of things in your own photos

- **PadCAD Lite:** An easy-to-use free CAD application designed for small to medium projects

WORLDS OF MAKING "MAKER" FRAMEWORK

CHOOSING THE RIGHT PRODUCTIONS FOR YOUR MAKERSPACE

M — Mobility
Does the product support free-range learning and liberate learners from the limitations of a physical makerspace, therefore increasing equity and access?

A — Allowance of Open-Ended Exploration
Is the product limited to step-by-step directions, or does it maximize inquiry by allowing the opportunity for open-ended exploration?

K — Knowledge of Student Needs, Wants, and Interests
Do you understand your learners? Does the product connect to the needs, wants, and interests of your students?

E — Empowerment and Engagement
Does the product empower *all* students by meeting them where they are? Does it have a low barrier of entry for engagement?

R — Relevance
Does the product have relevance to your school community and/or global trends and best practices?

Map Out Your Makerspace Action Plan

Work with your team to map out your plan for gathering the resources you need and want to support your themes. If you aren't ready to stock your makerspace yet, be sure to add your ideas to your Makerspace Action Plan for later use.

Theme	Materials/ Supplies	Books

Digital Resources (Websites)	Apps	People	Other

What Should You Buy for Your Makerspace?

Photo courtesy of Mongol Makers NGO, Mongolia

Having themes for your makerspace certainly streamlines the ordering process, but how do you know what to buy? I cannot possibly tell you what to buy for your makerspace, since you are designing a space that is unique to your school community, but in the following pages is the Worlds of Making MAKER Framework, a tool that will help you analyze with a critical lens the products you are considering for your makerspace, to guide your decision making. Your decision about whether or not to purchase a certain product for your makerspace should be based on how well the product meets the needs of your makerspace and your students. This is the framework I have always used to evaluate what I want to put in my makerspace, and I have also used it with districts all over the nation.

Mobility

In my opinion, next-generation makerspaces are mobile. Just as students no longer need to be tied to a computer lab, mobile technologies can liberate learners from the limitations of a physical makerspace; so you should build an environment and include resources that encourage tinkering, play, and open-ended exploration for everyone, anywhere, at any time. Equity and access are at the heart of ensuring that all students have available to them the opportunities that school makerspaces present. Many school libraries, for example, circulate makerspace-related materials for classroom teachers to use in their spaces or for students to make with at home. In addition, we see many makerspace activities popping up in school cafeterias, hallways, and outside.

Allowance of Open-Ended Exploration

Many makerspace products are limited to step-by-step directions and therefore do not allow for that open-ended exploration that is so important in a GREAT

makerspace. Students have opportunities to follow directions and make things all the time, so it is important that your makerspace experience differentiates from that and provides opportunities for students to take control of their own learning. For example, our Lego table contains bins of Legos, as well as directions for creating specific projects. This allows students the opportunity to engineer, design, and build their own creations.

KNOWLEDGE OF STUDENT NEEDS, WANTS, AND INTERESTS

So often I get asked the questions: What should I buy that will get my students excited? How do I know what my students will be interested in? My response is always ASK THEM! The first phase of the makerspace planning process is to understand your learners. It is important to take the time to understand your learners, to hear their voice, to give them a voice, and to connect your space and the products in it to their needs, wants, and interests. For example, one of our makerspace themes is computer coding. Supporting this theme with online tools and websites was easy, but when it came to purchasing the physical products to support that theme, it became a bit more challenging for me. As a result, I turned to my students and asked them what products they would be most interested in and what products would best support the things they wanted to make and create. The student input led me in directions I would not have necessarily gone myself. It ensured that the products we selected would be used and would be meaningful to the students.

EMPOWERMENT AND ENGAGEMENT

In my makerspace, I have what are called fixed stations and flexible stations. The fixed stations are products, materials, and activities that are out in my space at all times. The flexible stations are activities, resources, materials, and supplies that rotate in and out of the space. Oftentimes, these flexible stations need extra adult support, guidance, or modeling. However, the materials, resources, and supplies at the fixed stations—the ones that are out in the space at all times—have a low barrier of entry.

Photo courtesy of Mongol Makers NGO, Mongolia

For example, two of our fixed stations have been our Lego table and our littleBits bar. The products at these stations are easy enough for the students to get started with independently, maybe with the help of signage or prompts or modeling, but they meet students where they are, building on their own unique levels of prior knowledge. This has ensured that our makerspaces are inclusive, that they meet the needs of *all* our learners, and help build learner independence. There are huge differences between rigor and difficulty. It is possible that our students will still be challenged by these products. I look for products that have a low barrier of entry but also ones with which the sky is the limit, ones that allow my students to take their learning as deep as they would like. Products that meet students where they are not only are the most engaging but will help students feel empowered.

Relevance

When selecting products for your makerspace, you want to be sure they have relevant connections to your school community and the wider world. This is going to ensure that what the students learn transcends your makerspace. Oftentimes in our makerspace, I try to include products that our students will have experiences with outside of school. For example, I have integrated drones into our space. Drones might not be the right product for another school's makerspace, but our students benefit from having experience with them.

SELECTING THE RIGHT PRODUCTS FOR YOUR MAKERSPACE IS CRITICAL

Below are some questions to keep in mind while you look at the various makerspace products that are out there. It is not necessary to check off all these boxes for each and every product. It certainly is possible that what you have in your makerspace can touch on just some of these things. My rule of thumb for choosing products for my makerspace is that the majority of the boxes on this checklist should be checked off.

Mobility

☐ Does the product support free-range learning and liberate learners from the limitations of a physical makerspace, therefore increasing equity and access?

Allowance of Open-Ended Exploration

☐ Does the product maximize inquiry by allowing for open-ended exploration?

Knowledge of Student Needs, Wants, and Interests

☐ Does the product connect to the needs, wants, and interests of your students?

Empowerment and Engagement

☐ Does the product have a low barrier of entry for engagement?

Relevance

☐ Does the product have relevance to your school community and/or global trends and best practices?

Use this space to document your GREAT ideas!

I imagine . . .

Use this space to document your GREAT ideas!

Photo courtesy of Miracule Gavor, in Ghana

Photo courtesy of Heather Lister

Photo courtesy of Cyndi Felton

Photo courtesy of Melissa Torrence

Photo courtesy of
Tierra Linda Elementary School

Now that you've completed the makerspace planning process, it is time to consider what making in the makerspace will actually look like. Challenge your students with authentic project ideas, activities, and opportunities for reflection.

5 CREATING THE CONDITIONS TO INSPIRE!

CREATE THE CONDITIONS TO INSPIRE

A question I am frequently asked by schools that have makerspaces is:

> **How can we get more of our students engaged in our makerspaces?**

Even educators whose makerspaces have the most dynamic themes and the best supplies often struggle with making their spaces engaging to students. The instinct of an educator in these instances is to teach more. Many educators feel that their direct instruction is what is needed to engage students in making experiences. While I do believe there is a place for some instruction for skill building in a makerspace, I don't believe it is the only strategy that should be used to engage our students; nor is teacher-led instruction the only way we can encourage our students to be creative or innovative. Rather than forcing students to make, I think it is up to us as educators to create the conditions to inspire our students to *want* to make.

Making does not occur as a result of teaching. Create the conditions to inspire your learners to take risks and innovate.

As a result of much discussion surrounding this topic, I asked members of my personal learning network to participate in a Padlet by contributing their ideas for how they create the conditions to inspire in their makerspaces. Their responses can serve as inspiration for you and your team as you plan and create your makerspace.

They are as follows:

- Use lots of growth mindset read-alouds to model the maker mindset.

- My makerspace feels like a please-touch museum.

- I remind myself 459 times a day to get out of their way. It's like cultivating a flame: it needs air, space, and room to grow.

- Through library centers that include creation and technology and research skills centers

- Flexible, collaborative seating/furniture

- Lots of signage and prompts

- I make alongside them. Give them the freedom and voice to teach me. Innovator's mindset is key. Mistakes are essential to learning.

- Have student maker mentors.

- Fantastic Failures. We discuss learning from mistakes and growth mindset.

- All creations are recognized. Pictures are taken of the creations and put in a running slide show on the TV in the room.

- I give parameters and ideas. We follow the design process to help build ideas and focus.

- Open exploration is key—students create and solve their own challenges.

- Messiness is encouraged. Risks are encouraged.

- Use authentic literature as a springboard into all that is possible.

- By inviting experts into our space to serve as inspiration and mentors

- Allowing them to respond. Sometimes it's important for others to share their experiences so that risks can be taken through their own choice; writing, typing, taking a picture. #studentchoice #studentvoice

- By letting students know that our makerspace is a safe, comfortable, fun place where a kid can be a kid!

- Student collaboration with other schools/makerspaces

Photo courtesy of Heather Lister

- Show them you care, and you will inspire!

- Let students think about what they will create, explore, take risks, and create something different! It's okay to not get it right away!

- BY LISTENING

- Sometimes it's important for others to share their experiences so that risks can be taken.

- My students are learning and struggling through making mistakes, going back and figuring out what went wrong and how to fix it.

- Storing materials in kid-friendly ways

- Preserve the integrity and understand the value of informal learning.

- Get them to try new things.

- We created a "Maker Buffet" to allow our second graders to sample each space for a week. Then after, they will be able to choose where they want to go to find their passion and create.

- Rather than teacher, consider calling yourself something else, such as "Dream Consultants" like @techshop.

- Set up, manage, and run your makerspace like a startup.

- Ask questions to promote inquiry.

Dream Time!

Inspiration will run wild in your school community when you create the opportunity for your entire school to engage in the making process with "DRop Everything and Make" (DREAM). Try it in your school! Build a schoolwide culture of making!

Student Maker Mentors

Instead of direct instruction from a teacher in a makerspace, what about student maker mentors like the ones in the Singapore Polytechnic school library? Rather than having teachers in the center of their makerspace, they have student mentors who are there to assist, support, and encourage other students as they learn new skills for making things. Their role is to guide students in their

making, offer specific guidance, or run workshops in their areas of expertise; share their making successes and challenges; and help sustain student projects.

Mystery Guest Maker

Inspire your students to want to make by inviting a special guest maker! Open the walls of your makerspace and invite community members to share their expertise and demonstrate their skills. Your students will also love mystery guest makers!

Makerspace Menus

Much thought and care must be put into any program that involves making. Management of students and resources helps minimize time wasted during preparation, transitions, and cleanup. Makerspace menus can help you differentiate learning for your students while also encouraging independent exploration and creativity. Using design tools such as Canva.com, you can create menus of resources that students can immediately refer to while you are assisting their classmates. Long Island, New York, school librarian Kristina Holzweiss created makerspace menus for the themes and topics in their makerspace, including movie making, robotics, Osmo, digital making, DIY making, building and electronics, coding, and 3-D printing. Each menu offers a list of suggested websites, apps, and tech toys that students can choose from. Many students take these menus home with them so they can explore their learning beyond the school day.

Photo courtesy of Kristina Holzweiss

Photo courtesy of Jen Holberg

Help Wanted

In an authentic way, advertise in your makerspace for opportunities that seek the help of your makers!

Wisconsin library media specialist Jen Holberg made this eye-catching display to attract makers to her space. Her ads included help wanted for the following:

- An innovation intern to design and print a fidget

- An active, creative person to create a DDR experience with Makey Makey

- A magnetic circuitry innovator to create a littleBits inchworm

- A special person whose love of cookies and 3-D printing will meld to design and print a custom cookie cutter using Cookie Caster

- A motivated electrician apprentice to learn about and experiment with paper circuits

Photo courtesy of Laura Fleming

Photo courtesy of Laura Fleming

THE KICKSTART GUIDE TO MAKING GREAT MAKERSPACES

Transliterate Making

Makerspaces enable opportunities for students to create, explore, imagine, and build. What better springboard for that than stories? Stories fuel and ignite the imagination.

Makerspaces and STEM labs are not the same.

Many people associate makerspaces with only STEM-related activities, but literacy and making can go hand in hand. As I explained in my first book, my own entry point into the Maker Movement was through literacy, in which I combined storytelling with a range of transmedia techniques to create opportunities for making, creating, and exploring. An understanding of transliterate making, reading and writing, and making across multiple media platforms, is key to meeting the needs of our 21st century learners, and it can help to inject some STEAM into any makerspace.

Courtesy of PodPi

Young people today are surrounded by platforms and devices, even upon entering school, and are accustomed to those platforms being integrated, providing them with immersive experiences. However, many school makerspaces, despite being filled with technology, give students a disjointed experience. Connecting these devices, tools, materials, and platforms through storytelling allows us to meet our students where they are ready to learn.

The integration of literacy and storytelling into your students' makerspace experiences will help to build context around the tools, materials, and supplies they use and help to derive meaning from various types of making. The addition of technology allows making and creating to flow seamlessly from one media to the next.

Create experiences in your makerspace, not projects.

How can you easily integrate transliterate making into your makerspace?

- Allow your students opportunities to write and share stories in creative ways across diverse media in your makerspace.

- Merge storytelling and multiple literacies with the current crop of digital and networking technologies in your makerspace.

- Seek makerspace resources that have storytelling at their core, such as PodPi, which teaches students coding JavaScript and electronics through fun, engaging, and challenging comic book adventures.

In addition to the ideas you have already read, talk to your team and brainstorm ideas for how you will inspire your students to engage with your makerspace.

_____

_____

_____

_____

_____

_____

_____

_____

_____

_____

_____

_____

What Constitutes Making?

So you have your themes in place; have materials, resources, and supplies to support your themes; and have created the conditions to inspire your learners to want to make. Now you're probably wondering what kinds of lessons or activities to include in your space.

There is room in school makerspaces for all types of making, but it is important not to limit your students to just arts and crafts or STEM projects in which they must follow step-by-step directions or use a kit. When I ask myself the question, "What constitutes making?" I always fall back on my definition of a makerspace to guide my thinking and decision making.

Photo courtesy of Laura Fleming

> A makerspace is a unique learning environment that encourages tinkering, play, and open-ended exploration for all.

The opportunity for open-ended exploration is a key component of a GREAT makerspace. It is important to remember that project ideas and activities should not be thought of and created just by teachers and should not always come in a kit. Open-ended exploration demands an inquiry-based approach, which increases procedural knowledge.

It is possible to teach and model basic skills, then flip your makerspace, so that students can ideate and innovate. You can also set the stage for exploratory learning in your makerspace by fueling and sparking making and creating through "challenges." Our first makerspace challenge consisted of a rotting orange, one Makey Makey kit, and a handwritten sign that read, "An orange as a spacebar! What can you make?" This simple challenge set the stage for our makerspace and helped spark a culture of innovation.

Make Something That Does Something

A challenge that has been in our makerspace since the beginning is the brilliant slogan of littleBits: "Make something that does something."

This challenge is the perfect combination of ambiguous and motivating. It gives our students just enough creative spark to get started in our space.

Make It Work

Makerspaces can pop up practically anywhere there is a little space and curiosity. The Tinkering Lab in the Library Learning Commons at Kaechele Elementary School contains a rotating supply of items students can use independently to tinker, develop skills, explore circuitry, and engineer ideas, including this station in which students are given parts to put together to make something work!

Make Me Something, Anything . . .

Another one of our favorite makerspace challenges was inspired by high school English teacher Barton Keeler, who presented his students with the challenge, "Make me something, anything. . . ." The cornerstone of the challenge was to give his students supplies and let them loose to create something connected with what they had read in class that school year. The results of the challenge were astounding to him. He discovered the following:

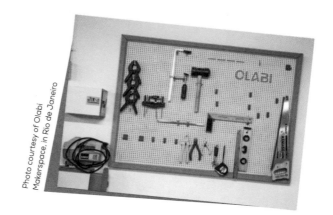

Photo courtesy of Olabi Makerspace, in Rio de Janeiro

- All the students were engaged from the first minute. The usual slow starters were quick to jump in.

- Student projects varied considerably; wide parameters spurred creativity.

- Students were taking their time; no one was doing it just to do it.

- Many students had ideas that involved time and resources out of class: stop-motion animation, Minecraft, video skits, and so forth.

- Students were accessing online resources to help with their projects.

What Else Can This Be?

Something I try to do in our makerspace through our challenges is help our students combat functional fixedness. Functional fixedness, or the inability to solve problems by using objects in new ways, has been proven to increase as people get older. This challenge can help students of all ages look at objects in your makerspace, as well as in the world, and think about other possible uses for them. It can even lead to the theme of upcycling in your makerspace. At Reed Elementary School in St. Louis, Missouri, students upcycled toilet-paper and paper-towel tubes and transformed them into cats, ninjas, hula dancers, pencil holders, and more!

They also upcycled cardboard boxes into FBI secret boxes, using the cardboard to create something fake that looked like the real thing (such as a book) that they could hide their valuables inside.

What Else Can You Make?

Erin Warzala, children's librarian at the Allen County Public Library in Indiana, created a challenge that was inspired by one of her favorite picture-book series. Recognizing that her makerspace is all about creativity, she left this challenge completely open, putting the book out for inspiration along with a tub of craft sticks, notched sticks, and old-fashioned clothespins.

What Can You Make With the Things in This Drawer?

When our makerspace first launched, I have to admit, I went out and bought kit after kit. There was something about our makerspace during that time that just didn't feel right to me. Our students didn't become better makers and certainly were not pushing their own creative limits. As time went on, I discovered that our students were being limited by the step-by-step directions that were included with the kits. Although we still buy some kits now, one of the things I do is break the kits apart and put a variety of the components into a bin in our makerspace that is labeled with the challenge, "What can you make with the things in this drawer?" This is definitely one of the most popular stations in our makerspace and oftentimes leads our students to do the most creative and innovative things.

When crafting a challenge for your makerspace, think in terms of giving students questions and not answers. Questioning is a powerful strategy for engaging your students in innovative thinking. Ask questions to spark and foster a culture of curiosity and thinking in your makerspace. Open-ended questions that promote higher-order thinking are inherently ambiguous and require more critical thinking and problem solving. Open-ended

Photo courtesy of Laura Fleming

Florida media specialist Tracey Mikos used this same challenge with her third graders. Their level of imagination was incredible.

Photo courtesy of Claudia Haines, nevershushed.com

questions typically begin with *what*, *why*, *how*, *describe*. For example, this can be something as simple as the challenge to the right, created by Alaskan librarian Claudia Haines.

Makerspace challenges written as open-ended questions transfer the making process onto the student, rather than limiting the possibilities for what the students might accomplish. Ultimately, teach students how to ask questions. Rather than always posting teacher-driven challenges in your makerspace, have your students craft challenges for themselves and their peers using open-ended questions. Take, for example, New Jersey educator Kristen Greco, who had her first-grade students explore makerspace materials so they could figure out the potential for

the materials and get the playing out of their system. As they did this, she asked them to be metacognitive and think about their thinking. She then asked them to formulate questions during interactive writing. The students came up with the thinking questions, "What [else] can I make?" and "How can I use this [material] in a new way?" The questions then sparked greater conversation, which she overheard and recorded in a chart called "Makerspace Talk." These overheard ideas show that her students began to think like makers, always ready to see the potential of new ideas in old objects.

Photo courtesy of Kristen Greco

Photo courtesy of Kristen Greco

Video Maker Challenges

Using videos in your makerspace is a great way to motivate students and to inspire them to think creatively. There is no limit to the types of videos or video clips that you can show to build schema or to spark creativity in your space. My students were inspired to design a school on Mars because of a video created by author and educator John Spencer. Each Thursday, John posts a new maker challenge to spark creative thinking with students, and you can subscribe at http://www.spencerauthor.com/challenge to receive each video in your inbox each week! My favorite video of his to date is his "Divergent Thinking Challenge: What would you make with this?" in which he says, "Don't forget to experiment and make tons of glorious mistakes!"

SCAMPER

In addition, I often use an online creative tool called SCAMPER to craft maker-space challenges that empower my students to stretch their thinking and making skills by encouraging them to generate new ideas or think about how to improve on existing ones. SCAMPER is a mnemonic device:

Substitute: Replace a part of something or of a process. What can be used instead?

Combine: Blend or bring together two or more unrelated materials in a new way. How can you combine materials to make something more useful or more interesting?

Adapt: Borrow, emulate, adapt, or amend an existing idea or thing.

Modify: How can you switch up the shape, size, color, or texture of something? How can you expand, augment, or intensify?

Put to another use: Can you use something for something else, or for more than one thing? Can you use it in a new way?

Eliminate: Streamline, simplify, or minimize. What can you remove or improve on to enhance a creation?

Rearrange or (**R**everse): Can parts of something be interchanged, inverted, or transposed? Can the sequence be switched up? Could you make a plan beginning with the desired outcome and design the steps leading up to it in reverse order? Can you reverse engineer something?

The anatomy of a good challenge:

- It is inspirational.

- It serves as a call to action and oftentimes is most effective if an imperative verb is used.

- It is open-ended and slightly ambiguous in nature.

- It is not dictated by one particular process; students can choose the process.

Photo courtesy of Olabi Makerspace, in Rio de Janeiro

Participatory Making

In addition to teacher-created challenges and activities in a makerspace, there is an opportunity to invite students into the design process. Students and teachers can be co-designers of student-centered learning experiences. Findings show that including students in the design of materials can provide curriculum designers with tools for creating materials that support students and teachers as co-designers and co-evaluators of the enacted curriculum that enhances teaching and learning for understanding.[1] This approach in a makerspace learning environment is what I call participatory making: including student voice and input in designing makerspace experiences, thereby making students co-creators and fostering student agency.

In collaboration with New Jersey educator Billy Krakower, I recently put the idea of participatory making into practice during a unit surrounding the new littleBits Code Kit. Billy and I were thrilled to be selected as one of 20 participants in the littleBits Lead Educator program, which gave us the opportunity to test the kit with students prior to its public release. We also were tasked with creating resources and activities that would be made available to the littleBits community.

Full disclosure . . . the students in my makerspace do not like kits. My students have been known to throw away directions, disassemble kits, and void warranties. With that being said, in partnership with my school's computer science teacher,

---

[1]Gunckel, K. L., & Moore, F. M. (2005). *Including students and teachers in the co-design of the enacted curriculum*. Paper presented at the NARST 2005 Annual Meeting, Dallas, TX. Retrieved from http://www.project2061.org/research/ccms/site.archive/documents/codesign_of_the_enacted_curriculum.pdf.

Ms. Kirsten Lee, and her AP Computer Science students, we were excited to be able to beta test the new littleBits Code Kit. Rather than designing lessons surrounding the littleBits Code Kit myself, I tasked my students with designing experiences they felt other students would enjoy, embrace, and benefit from. The ultimate goal of our littleBits collaboration was for my students to create an activity for Billy's third- and fourth-grade students to complete and to share with the littleBits community as well.

Photo courtesy of Laura Fleming

I first immersed my students in this unit by having them watch the "Building Blocks That Blink, Beep, and Teach" TED Talk given by the founder of littleBits, Ayah Bdeir. Students also read an article called "Game Changer" written by Tyler Winegarner for *Make:* magazine and gained a better understanding of how to craft immersive experiences. Students then did some research to answer the following guiding question:

> **What techniques can be used to better engage students with makerspace kits, such as the littleBits Code Kit?**

Some of their findings:

- In our current generation, video games have increased in popularity, really becoming a staple in our current culture. When making kits, one of the focuses should be storytelling. With a good story, players make connections to the characters and an overall connection to the kit itself. Storytelling creates an emotional investment in the kit. Think about it: Without an emotional connection, why would you care about something?

- To better engage students, self-directed learning could be encouraged by the people who make the kits. The kit would allow for the proper environment for self-directed learning to take place. Kits such as littleBits have so many possibilities and offer so many opportunities that allowing for self-directed learning will allow people to discover things and to learn about themselves and their needs too.

- Storytelling helps the people in an experience feel more engaged and a part of it. It plays into the emotion of the user and makes more of a connection. The user can relate to the games and makes them feel like they are truly part of the game.

- Gamification can be used to make the kits feel more immersive. By making the kits more game-like, kids are more likely to be engaged and be interested; they will see the kits less as learning and more as fun.

My students were then ready to put on their experience designer hats. At the same time, Billy's students were also diving in deep with the littleBits Code Kit, honing their skills in order to successfully test the experiences created by my students. My students took all they learned and applied it to crafting experiences surrounding the littleBits Code Kit, which they then sent to Billy's students, who helped my students refine and debug their work, ultimately improving the experiences my students created.

As a result of the participatory making opportunities afforded to my students in this littleBits Code Kit unit, they recommend the following tips to other students who are doing the same:

- Show, rather than tell, examples of what you can do with makerspace items.

- Create a forum where students who create in your makerspace can collaborate and share what they have created.

- Build in choice. Create experiences similar to pick-your-path books. This puts the power of creativity into the hands of the students.

Inviting students into the makerspace activity design process can be transformative for your space. Participatory making experiences, such as the ones our students experienced, are sure to empower your students and help to guarantee your makerspace is the student-driven space we ultimately want those spaces to be.

CHALLENGE YOURSELF!

Using the anatomy of a GREAT makerspace challenge as a guide, along with the SCAMPER creative tool, work with your team to brainstorm possible makerspace challenges.

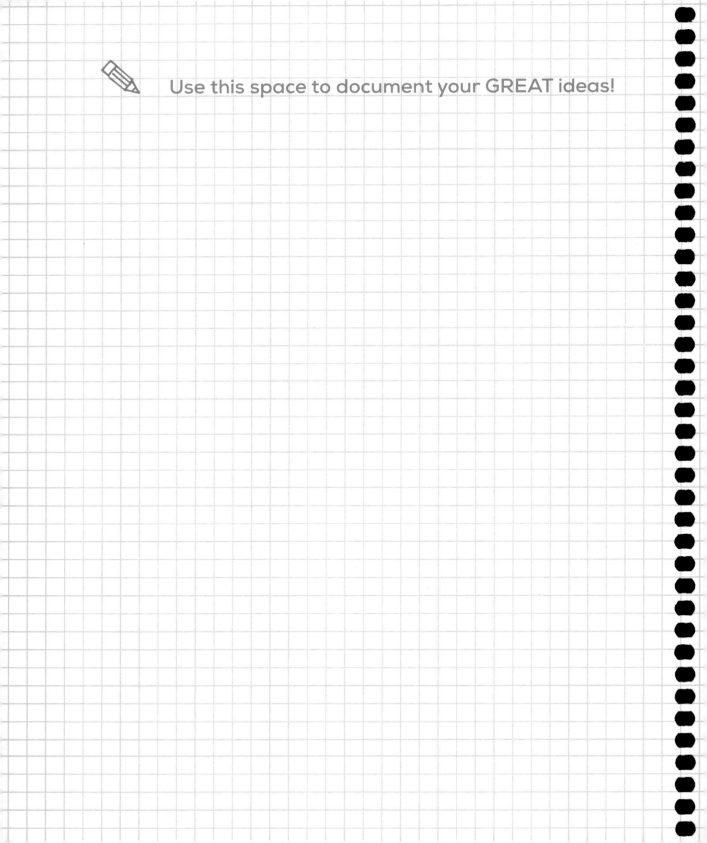

Use this space to document your GREAT ideas!

I imagine . . .

Use this space to document your GREAT ideas!

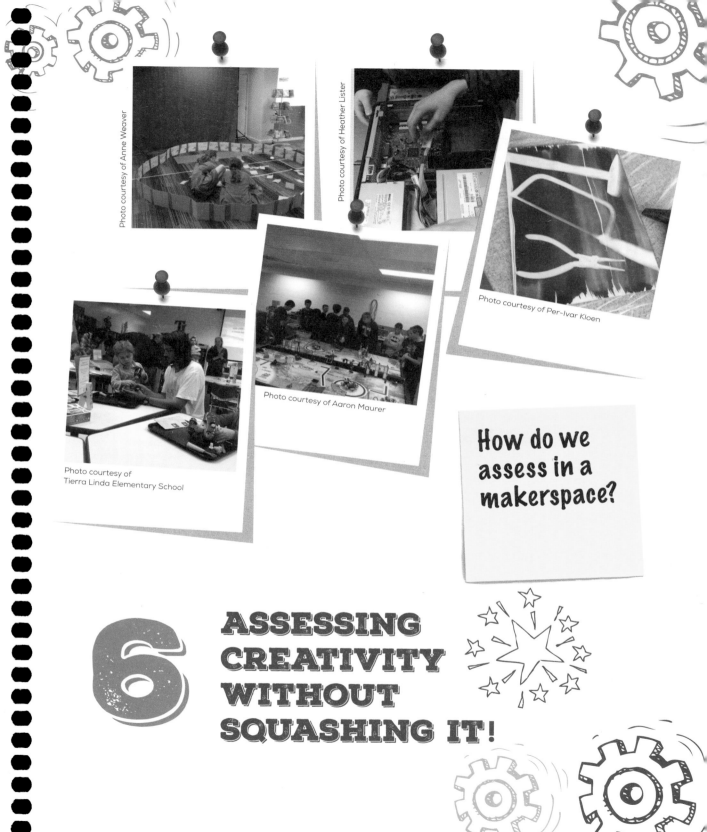

Photo courtesy of Anne Weaver

Photo courtesy of Heather Lister

Photo courtesy of Per-Ivar Kloen

Photo courtesy of Aaron Maurer

Photo courtesy of
Tierra Linda Elementary School

How do we assess in a makerspace?

6 ASSESSING CREATIVITY WITHOUT SQUASHING IT!

FLIPPING ASSESSMENT IN A MAKERSPACE ON ITS HEAD

Many educators and school leaders wonder how students can be appropriately assessed in maker environments. One of the questions I am asked most frequently is:

> **How do we assess in a makerspace?**

In my book *Worlds of Making: Best Practices for Establishing a Makerspace for Your School*, I touch on assessment and say that a makerspace can have activities associated with the standards and those activities can even be assessed; however, making doesn't always have to be—indeed, I would argue, *must* not always be—tied to traditional assessment. All too common is the mindset that traditional methods of assessment are the only valid means to measure learning.

Because many school makerspaces are informal and unique learning environments, they demand unique assessment methods.

> **BRING MAKERSPACES INTO CLASSROOMS. DON'T BRING CLASSROOMS INTO MAKERSPACES.**

A mindset shift is needed to discover and embrace assessment methods that allow for the iteration, failure, collaboration, and messiness that makerspaces are all about. Assessment in a makerspace should be flipped on its head. It should be altered so profoundly that up is down, left is right, and a person's experience and expectations have been completely transformed. This is the kind of assessment our makerspaces need.

Rather than formalizing a makerspace so much that it becomes a classroom, consider nontraditional methods of assessment that give students credit for the skills they gain in your space, celebrate those accomplishments, and validate that learning. My own students will tell you that the last thing they want is to be assessed in the traditional sense on what they do in our makerspace, but at the same time, they want credit for the skills they gain.

We know that in a makerspace, one size does not fit all; therefore, it is important to find flexible assessment models that can be responsive to the learning that is taking place in your space. Traditional education typically relies on assessments that measure success; however, in a makerspace, the iterative process, which may include failure, should also be celebrated. In addition, it is important that you and your makerspace planning team consider ways to acknowledge the granular skills students will gain in your makerspace, as well as "soft skills"—such as teamwork and communication—that normally fall outside the scope of traditional assessments.

When deciding on assessment methods for your makerspace, your makerspace planning team should consider the following characteristics of effective makerspace assessments:

- ☐ Be responsive
- ☐ Embrace the iterative process
- ☐ Acknowledge skills the students gain
- ☐ Capture the process, not just the product

Formative assessments such as exit interviews, surveys, and portfolios have proven successful in school makerspaces. In addition, assessment methods that are qualitative in nature, such as teachers' listening to conversation and makerspace talk, can provide feedback that is equally effective. Educator Kristopher Velez from Mumbai, India, has students share their DIY/Maker plans on Instructables.com for community feedback, as a form of authentic assessment.

Digital Badging

As a result of my students' requests, we have begun using micro credentials in the form of digital badges in our makerspace. These badges acknowledge the skills students gain in our space and have helped build a culture of recognition in our school community. In addition, badges that students earn can be uploaded to résumés, included with college applications, embedded into websites or blogs, or shared across social media.

To earn a digital badge in our space, students must provide evidence that they have successfully met the criteria for earning that badge. The digital badges the students earn are "clickable," allowing anyone to see the description of the badge, as well as the criteria for earning it.

Some of our digital badges are related to 3-D printing and design. Below are two of them, along with the metadata behind them.

Title
3-D Modeling

Description
The earner of this badge has demonstrated proficiency in designing and printing ideas and digital creations.

Criteria
In order to earn this badge, the badge earner has demonstrated a working knowledge of the fundamentals of designing 3-D files using software of choice, such as Tinkercad, Adobe SketchUp, Meshmixer, and/or AutoCAO. Earners of this badge successfully have produced a unique 3-D design using software of choice and export for 3-D printing. Earners also have used preexisting designs, imported to software of choice and exported for printing.

Issuer
Worlds of Learning

Issue Date
05/31

Title
3-D Printing Troubleshooting

Description
Earners of this badge have demonstrated proficiency in troubleshooting 3-D designs and printing issues.

Criteria
Earners of this badge have demonstrated that they can remove any material from clogged extruders. In addition, the badge earner knows how to stop 3-D printer if an unwanted operation were to occur. They also have printed prototypes and have demonstrated the ability to improve upon 3-D models to increase the quality of 3-D designs and prints.

Issuer
Worlds of Learning

Issue Date
05/31

Digital badges are flexible enough to recognize skills that fall outside of traditional assessments. They are a powerful tool for capturing and telling the story of a student's entire learning and can paint a more meaningful picture of what a student knows, beyond a test score or a letter grade. In your makerspace, you can use digital badges as the foundation for a system in which students can take control of their learning and learn what they want to learn when they want to learn it. Digital badges also open the door for community partnerships with local businesses that might endorse the badges, potentially adding to their credibility, validity, and clout.

Interested in digital badges for your makerspace? I use a tool called Credly to create my digital badges; however, there are lots of free tools out there. In addition, many learning management systems now allow you to easily create digital badges and issue them to your students. **Discuss with your makerspace planning team the following points:**

Photo courtesy of Per-Ivar Kloen

- Where will you create badges?

- How will you issue badges?

- What incentive will your students have for wanting to earn a badge?

- Where will students keep their badges after they earn them?

- How will students share evidence with you to earn the badge?

Whether or not you use digital badges in your makerspace, let them serve as the starting point for a conversation with your team about if and how you will assess in your makerspace.

DEVELOP
YOUR OWN BADGES

Use this sheet to work with your team and think through a possible badge for your makerspace. Discuss with your team the badge's purpose and value. Consider developing a series of badges per skill, allowing the students the opportunity to "level up" and continue to build on their skills.

Badge name

Standards addressed by this badge (optional)

Badge criteria: What does a student need to do to earn the badge?

Badge design: What do you want this badge to look like?

Description: What skills or knowledge does this badge represent?

Evidence: What does the student have to demonstrate to show that he or she has met the skills outlined in the badge?

Maryland media specialist Nan Stifel uses digital badges as part of student portfolios, as a means of assessing the maker work of her students. Using Seesaw for Schools, her third-grade students scan a QR code to access their library/maker portfolios on iPads. They add "artifacts" to their portfolios—photos, videos, links to websites, and so forth—and reflect or comment on those items. Students save items, then Nan reviews them and approves them for sharing with parents via an e-mail generated by the app. Parents have access only to their own child's portfolio.

In reviewing the added artifacts, Nan tags them with specific skills she has identified as student learning goals for maker- and library-related projects. For example, the first time a student uses the Do Ink green screen app to produce a video book review, the associated artifact is tagged with one star for that skill. Repeated practice and mastery of that skill result in additional stars. When a student has earned four stars for a particular skill or tool, he or she is awarded a digital badge for that skill or tool. The badges, created by Nan, are placed in the student's "Badges" Seesaw folder with a congratulatory note.

Sample badges the teacher may put in the student's "Badges" folder
Created by Nan Stifel

As she starts to tag skills with younger grades, the students will develop a maker portfolio that will carry over to the next grade. The prospect of developing cumulative portfolios that document building projects, collaborative design, woodworking proficiencies, robotics, and other makerspace STEAM activities is exciting to Nan, as the portfolios will reflect student achievement and justify the maker curriculum. Whether the badging system will be beneficial as the students move on to their next schools is unknown at this point, but at the very least, the badges are a source of great pride for the 9-year-olds.

	Collaborative Design Challenge: LEGO, etc.	Collaborative Design Challenge: Snap Circuits	Design/Build with Rigamajig	Doink Green Screen	Safe Internet Searching for Information or Images	Scroll Saw	Seesaw app entries and reflection	Woodworking with Hand Tools
A 🐬	3	0	3	2	1	1	3	1
A 🐌	2	1	2	1	1	0	2	0
B 🐗	1	1	1	1	1	0	3	0
C 🐬	0	1	1	2	1	0	2	1
C 🐶	2	0	1	2	1	0	3	1

The "Skills View" allows the teacher to track student progress. The numbers in the blocks refer to the number of artifacts tagged with a specific skill. The colors refer to the continuum of proficiency: red = one star, yellow = two stars, light green = three stars, dark green = four stars.

Created by Nan Stifel

Although Nan's focus at Concord Hill School is early childhood, the Seesaw app may be used for older students as well, using shared or 1:1 devices and QR code logins or e-mail or Google account logins.

Reflections

Another way to assess in a makerspace is to have the students reflect on their making experiences. Reflections are a way to track progress and communicate learning. They can be a powerful method for assessing performance in a makerspace and can help our students grow from their experiences. Not only is the reflection process an important tool for students to construct meaning from their makerspace experiences, but it also enables educators to better shape their makerspaces based on the feedback gained from student reflections. For example, you might be able to identify certain skills that a student needs to develop and therefore that you need to focus on in your space.

Reflection can take many forms. Students in your makerspace might consider keeping a journal in which they document their making experiences. Reflections can also be done as videos to be shared with peers, family and friends, or a more authentic audience. At the Qualcomm Thinkabit Lab, in California, students leave reflections on their writable glass tables. Long Island, New York, school librarian Kristina Holzweiss has her students reflect on their making using "I'm a Maker, Not a Consumer" signs. Students choose to celebrate any part of the creation process by explaining what they learned during a particular session. They may choose to explain what they learned, the progress they are making on their project, or even

Photo courtesy of Kellyanne Burbage

the personal and interpersonal skills they have developed. Students then use these signs as prompts for Flipgrid interviews. Kellyanne Burbage, Sangaree Intermediate school librarian in South Carolina, has her students reflect on their making experiences using maker notebooks. The notebooks are made from construction paper and graph paper. At the end of the week, students spend time writing in their notebooks: what worked or didn't, what they want to try next. They include sketches, too.

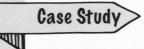

Case Study

Makerspace Stories and Social Media: Leveraging the Learning

By Ross Cooper and Laura Fleming

By assigning students a one-minute, social-media-friendly video reflecting on their makerspace experience, you encourage them to bring their learning into the world where they live.

The maker movement is built upon a constructivist philosophy that views learning as a highly personal and social process. In this philosophy, teachers facilitate inquiry-based learning, student development of knowledge and thinking processes, and student interaction and sharing of ideas.

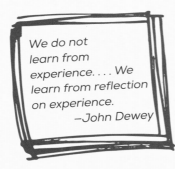

> We do not learn from experience. . . . We learn from reflection on experience.
> —John Dewey

Reflection and sharing are core components of inquiry, which should be pervasive in all makerspaces. (According to the Buck Institute, reflection is one of the seven essential elements of project-based learning, which falls under the umbrella of inquiry-based learning, http://www .bie.org.) As educators, we can build student capacity to reflect upon the making process, and then be intentional about finding and creating opportunities for students to reflect, share, and celebrate their experiences. Reflection skills and strategies can turn inquiry into a natural part of the making process, as opposed to simply tacking on reflection after the fact because "we were told it's important."

Learning that endures should transcend a makerspace. Adding social media tools such as Snapchat and Instagram to the context of making can give students a channel for displaying their experiences by communicating what they have accomplished with a large, diverse audience. Social media platforms enable many engaging classroom activities, including "communities of practice" where learners can interact and share ideas. Reflection with video on these platforms, as well as peer feedback, can highlight the making process in a way that builds student voice and agency in an online environment.

Furthermore, there is tremendous value in utilizing authentic tools and platforms that are already part of students' personal (and possibly, educational) lives. According to Superintendent Joe Sanfelippo of Fall

Creek School District in Wisconsin, "If schools access the spaces where students and parents live virtually, we are definitely in a place that we can leverage. It gives us a common forum and meets users on their turf, not ours." In addition, rather than "locking and blocking" these tools, we should be proactively teaching students how to use them effectively and appropriately. (After all, no matter how much a school pretends that they don't exist, students *will* use them.) As Ross used to tell his fourth-grade students, "In middle and high school, when all of your friends are messing around on social media, I want you to be using it to grow your own businesses!"

With these thoughts in mind, use the rest of this post to help your students reflect upon their makerspace experiences and tell their stories using Snapchat Stories—**Makerstories**—and Instagram (or Instagram Stories)—**Makergrams**!

Learning Plan

Using Snapchat or Instagram, create a one-minute video in which you reflect upon your makerspace experience. Decide on the components that will best tell your story. You can use the criteria below as a starting point, but ultimately you should decide how to apply it to your own work. Do your best to keep moving toward developing your own criteria for your video reflections!

1. Essential Question (10 seconds)

What was the overarching question that you explored or the question that drove your recent work? What question formed your maker journey? Example: "How can I use aerodynamics to make my Lego car travel faster?"

2. Iterative Process (25 seconds)

We want the process, not necessarily the product, to be the main focus of our work. Here are some prompts to guide you:

- What did I make/do? (Describe your prototype.) Example: "I designed an aerodynamic hood to be 3-D printed and attached to a Lego car that I built."

(Continued)

(Continued)

- What materials did I use/work with? Example: "I designed my object in Tinkercad and printed it out on our 3-D printer."

- What surprised me during the process? Example: "I was surprised with how many times I had to go back and improve my prototype design."

- What frustrations did I experience? Example: "Even after a few improvements on the design of my object, I just couldn't get it right. My car wasn't traveling any faster."

- What about your initial prototype ended up being successful? Example: "Finally, after adjusting the angles of my design, I was successful because it made my Lego car travel faster."

3. Enduring Understanding(s) (10 seconds)

As a result of your experience, what do you now understand/know? What are you now able to do? Example: "By using the principles of aerodynamics, I was able to increase the speed at which my Lego car traveled. I was able to see how aerodynamics increase the speed of an object by reducing drag."

4. Reflection (15 seconds)

Here are some prompts to guide you:

- Did I achieve my goal? Why or why not?

- Along the way, what changes did I have to make to meet my goal?

- What changes will I make the next time I engage in a similar process?

- Here's a call to action for my peers.

Here's an example of a reflection: "The next time I design an object, I'll design it first on paper or cut out of cardboard, and then digitally. I feel this will decrease the number of times that I have to print out my prototype. Try that out the next time you're designing an object. And be sure to let me know what you think about what I made!"

A Few Additional Points

- In addition to having students create video reflections, consider providing them with starting points for how to respond to each other's work once it's posted on social media. (For example, how to leave appropriate feedback is an entire lesson in and of itself.)

- The one-minute requirement for video pushes students to
  - prioritize their most pertinent information, and
  - exercise their creativity within this time constraint.

- According to public speaking coach and author Carmine Gallo, "Great communicators reach your head and touch your heart. Most people who deliver a presentation forget the 'heart' part." If you want to reach people's minds *and* hearts, tell a story. While Makerstories and Makergrams may contain data, facts, and analysis, they also include narratives, which can get viewers emotionally invested in the learning.

- Encourage students to explore self-expression and creativity through their stories using different features of the video platforms, such as filters, emojis, drawing, and text.

- Snapchat and Instagram Stories will disappear after 24 hours, but they can be saved to the device on which they're created. (However, as of now, Instagram Stories can only be downloaded one photo or video at a time unless you use the Chrome IG Story extension.) For more on Snapchat, check out A. J. Juliani's *Complete Guide to Snapchat for Teachers and Parents*. For more on Instagram Stories, check out the official Instagram Help Center.

While we've designed guidelines for creating the Makerstories and Makergrams, we'd ultimately like students to progress toward developing their own criteria for video reflections. Much like how inquiry-based learning calls for students to formulate their own questions, students should *also* generate the criteria that most effectively tell their stories. Starting with our suggested framework and gradually transferring responsibility onto your students will help them begin to make critical thinking and reflection innate components of their making process.

Source: *Makerspace Stories and Social Media: Leveraging the Learning*. Edutopia by Ross Cooper and Laura Fleming. (Originally published September 1, 2016 © Edutopia.org; George Lucas Educational Foundation.)

Looking Ahead

Congratulations! You have made it to the end of our kickstart guide for making GREAT makerspaces. To ensure the sustainability of your makerspace, as well as the maker movement, it is important to understand that makerspaces are never finished. Revisit the makerspace planning process at least one time per school year to reevaluate your makerspace themes. Based on the data you collect from the phases of the planning process, you might find themes you want to add, drop, or put on the back burner.

Not only do we want to instill a growth mindset in the students who visit our makerspace, but we as educators need to have that same growth mindset. Some things you plan for your makerspace will be successful; some things will not. It is essential that you take the time to reflect on your space to make necessary changes. This will ensure that your space is not only vibrant for now but also sustainable into the future.

And finally, let's stay connected and continue to learn from each other, like the educators at the École Sir John A. Macdonald Public School in Kingston, Ontario, Canada, did!

Photo courtesy of Jennifer Banham

MAKERSPACE
REFLECTION FORM

Back Then

Right Now

Next School Year

Share your makerspace experiences and what you'd like to try! Tweet your thoughts with the hashtag #makingGREATmakerspaces!

HAPPY MAKING!

Photo courtesy of Per-Ivar Kloen

I imagine . . .

OK!

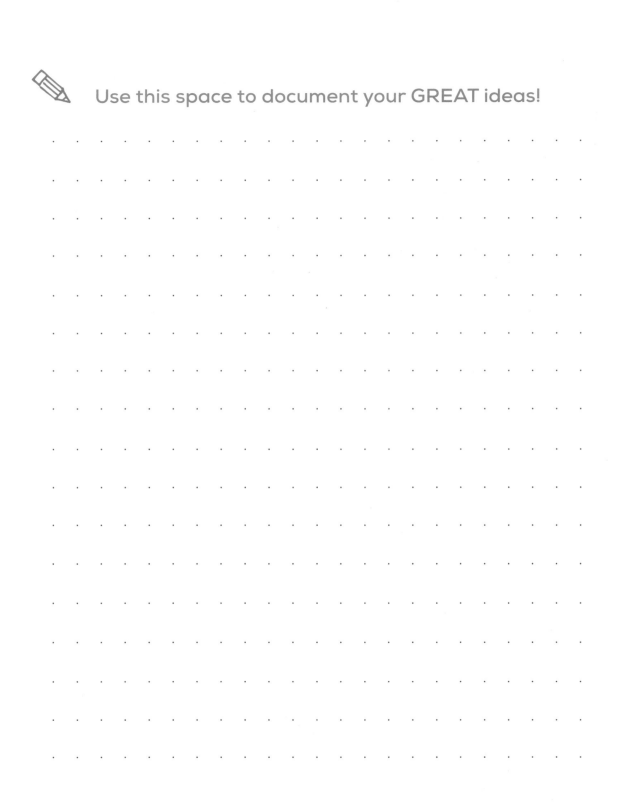

Use this space to document your GREAT ideas!

Index

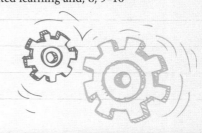

A SAGE Publishing Company

Helping educators make the greatest impact

CORWIN HAS ONE MISSION: to enhance education through intentional professional learning.

We build long-term relationships with our authors, educators, clients, and associations who partner with us to develop and continuously improve the best evidence-based practices that establish and support lifelong learning.